ON THE ROAD
WITH JESUS

BEN WITHERINGTON III

❖

ON THE ROAD
WITH JESUS

TEACHING AND HEALING

Abingdon Press
Nashville

ON THE ROAD WITH JESUS
TEACHING AND HEALING

Copyright © 2012 by Abingdon Press

All rights reserved.

This book is printed on acid-free paper.

Library of Congress Cataloging-in-Publication Data

Witherington, Ben, 1951–
    On the road with Jesus : teaching and healing / Ben Witherington III.
        p.   cm.
    ISBN 978-1-4267-1216-6 (trade pbk. : alk. paper)
    1. Jesus Christ—Person and offices.   2. Bible. N.T. Gospels—Criticism, interpretation, etc.   I. Title.
    BT203.W58   2012
    232.9'5—dc23

                                                                          2011040151

All scripture quotations are the author's own translation.

12 13 14 15 16 17 18 19 20 21—10 9 8 7 6 5 4 3 2 1

MANUFACTURED IN THE UNITED STATES OF AMERICA

CONTENTS

PREFACE

The further one gets into the life and ministry of Jesus, the clearer it becomes what a complex person Jesus was. It also becomes apparent how challenging his words and deeds were, not merely for those who were antagonistic but even for his own disciples. In this volume of our series, we will be exploring Jesus' Galilean ministry in some detail and looking at the way Jesus presented himself to the peoples of his own region.

In the first chapter we will focus on Jesus the person and look at him as a seer, a sage, and a healer. In the last chapter, we will consider the messianic side of who he was. What did it mean to call him the Messiah, the anointed one of God? In the two middle chapters, we will look at the Sermon on the Mount, an essential summary of some of Jesus' core teachings, and then we will examine some of Jesus' relationships: with John the Baptizer, with the Pharisees, with the Sadducees, and with the Zealots. Along the way, as we travel down the road with Jesus, eventually heading to Jerusalem and his date with destiny, we will reflect on the significance of all this material for faith in Jesus today.

The four DVD sessions that go with this guidebook are not intended to duplicate the four chapters in this book but to supplement them so the reader will have a more detailed contextual understanding of the Gospels. As I like to put it, a text without a context is just a pretext for whatever one wants it to mean. Studying the life of Jesus in its original historical, archaeological, social, and religious contexts helps us rule in and rule out certain ways of interpreting the Man who Fits No One Formula: Jesus of Nazareth.

Christmas 2011

CHAPTER ONE

JESUS THE SEER, THE SAVIOR, THE SAGE

The parables were dark sayings meant to tease the mind into active thought about the Kingdom.

—C. H. Dodd

O YOUNG AND FEARLESS PROPHET

One of the main reasons John the Baptizer surprised people is that some Jews of his time thought there were no more prophets in the land, and that there had not been for some time. John caused people to reassess, so that when Jesus came on the scene, the buzz was that perhaps he was a prophet as well, a prophet like John. And after John died, somebody even suggested he was John back from the dead (see Mark 8:28)! But there were prophets and then there were prophets—one size did not fit all. In fact there was a northern style of prophet, and there was a southern style of prophet, and if one came from Galilee, the natural assumption would be that a prophet would be like Elijah, who along with Elisha, ministered to the northern tribes, to Israel rather than to Judah. If we analyze the chronicles of the ministries of Elijah and Elisha what we mainly find are two action prophets—prophets noted for miracles for the people and for sticking their noses in the political business of royalty. At least in regard to the former, Jesus appeared to be like Elijah. Elijah, after all, had also brought back someone from the dead. And Jesus had called the ruler of Galilee, Herod Antipas, "that fox" and was critical of his marriage and his treatment of John the Baptizer, and rightly so.

Judaean prophets in the classical mode were oracular prophets. They would hear a late word from God, and then quote it verbatim, often using the "thus says Yahweh..." formula. They were mouthpieces who had a good earpiece tuned into God's frequency. This was clearly not Jesus' modus operandi. Not once does he speak as a mere mouthpiece for the Father. And because of this, some have suggested Jesus was not a prophet. The problem with that conclusion is that Jesus even calls himself a prophet more than once (for example, in Mark 6).

We need to expand our horizons and realize that there were classical prophets and there were action prophets, there were parable-telling prophets (see Nathan and his confrontation with David), and there were apocalyptic seers. If we have to characterize Jesus, he was like all of these sorts of prophets, except the classical prophets. He told parables, he confronted authorities, he performed miracles, and yes, he had visions. We have already discussed the latter when we investigated his baptism and his early temptations in the wilderness.[1] Jesus was a man who fit no one single prophetic formula or stereotype, but a prophet and a seer he was.[2]

But of course Jesus was both more and other than a prophet. John, so far as we know, performed no miracles, but Jesus performed miracles no one had seen before in Judaism, specifically the healing of a man born blind (we have no such story in the Old Testament or intertestamental Judaism[3]) and many, many exorcisms, another miracle nowhere recorded in the Old Testament. Furthermore, no one had heard of someone being raised from the dead after they had lain in the grave for four days and had started to decompose. Jesus even did that in the case of Lazarus, and what was so astonishing about that is that Jewish tradition said that the spirit of a person departed into the afterlife after three days. They weren't coming back after that. There was, however, another side to who Jesus was. He was not just a seer, he was also a sage, a teacher of wisdom, and we need to talk about this side of his ministry as well.[4] Jesus' miracles were performed in the context of working as a messianic prophet and a messianic sage. He was indeed a man who could not be pigeonholed.

THE MIGHTY WORKS OF A MIGHTY MAN

There are two traditions about Jesus' miracles, a northern tradition and a southern tradition. In Judaea, Jesus was primarily noted for performing "sign miracles," that is miracles that had high symbolic content that pointed away from themselves to the one performing the sign. They were signs that the king had come. In Galilee, Jesus performed "mighty works," which were indicators that the Kingdom, or Dominion, had arrived. The former included dramatic healings and raisings from the dead and even judging miracles (for example, the cursing of the fig tree) but no exorcisms. The latter included every kind of miracle imaginable: healings, raisings, nature miracles, exorcisms; you name it, Jesus could do it. It is interesting that in the Synoptic Gospels the miracles are called "mighty works" (*dunameis*, from which we get the word *dynamite!*) whereas in John they are called *semeion*, emphasizing not so much their power as their symbolic character.

If we examine closely the miracle traditions in the four Gospels, there are a variety of things that stand out. In Mark's Gospel, particularly in its first half, exorcisms seem to be the most prevalent miracle along with healings, whereas in the Fourth Gospel and in Judaea, it's a different story. The second thing to note is that Jesus does not perform miracles using magic or sacred formulae or recipes, unlike others who claimed to do miracles in his era. Jesus does not do miracles on the basis of someone else's authority or power, but on the basis of his own. Right from the start in Galilee when he heals the man with the "unclean spirit" (that is, a spirit that made the man unclean) the crowds in the synagogue in Capernaum are amazed and note that Jesus seems to have independent, or personal authority, not derived power and authority. In a culture where it was assumed that only God had inherent power and authority, this was shocking. The third thing to notice about Jesus' miracles is they are largely effortless. Jesus doesn't have to wrestle with demons in a cage match or go through a prolonged process of healing; however, at least once he chooses to heal a man in stages. Several times he has the one being healed participate in his or her own curative process ("Go wash," he says to the blind man. "Go see the priest," he says to the man he has made clean). Jesus can even heal at a distance and does so even for foreigners like a Syrophoenician woman or a centurion near Cana.

A further point worth emphasizing strongly is that Jesus does not see miracle-working as his main task. Early in Mark's Gospel, he tells his disciples he needs to get away from Capernaum for a while; and so he tells them, "Let us go on to the neighboring towns, so that I may proclaim the message there also; *for that is what I came out to do*" (Mark 1:38). Jesus went out to proclaim his Dominion message about salvation, and he stayed to heal. He did not set out to do a bunch of healings; he was merely responding to great human need. This is an important point in regard to Jesus' priorities. If someone is saved and has the divine saving rule of God in his or her life, that person has an everlasting benefit from Jesus. But even the man raised from the dead is still a mortal man and will go on to die again. Jesus knew what his priorities needed to be, and the emphasis was on the message, the good news of salvation, and its reception by faith. The miracles were part of the salvation package to be sure, but not the main thing. The miracles were acts of compassion, but they were not Jesus' main passion, which was to rescue the lost.

One of the more interesting subjects to study in the Gospels is the relationship of faith to miracles. There seems to be a positive correlation between faith in the miracle worker and the possibility of healing. We see this for instance in the famous story of the woman with the perpetual flow of blood. Jesus tells her quite clearly at the end of the story—"your faith has healed you" (Mark 5:34). And on the opposite end of the spectrum Mark 6:5 says of Nazareth, "And he could do no mighty works there except that he laid hands on a few sick people and cured them. And he was amazed at their unbelief." The problem in Nazareth like the problem with Thomas in John's Gospel is unbelief, not doubting.

There seem to be certain kinds of miracles that got Jesus into real hot water: exorcisms, which led to the charge that he was in league with Satan (see Mark 3), and "unnecessary" healings on the Sabbath. The rule about the Sabbath was no nonemergency work on that day, so if a healing could wait until after sundown on Saturday, then it should wait. Jesus, to the contrary, saw the Sabbath, the day of rest, as the perfect day to give a person rest from what ailed him or her, and in all the differing layers of the Gospel tradition, Jesus is portrayed as healing various people with various maladies, including non-life-threatening ones, on the Sabbath. Jesus did quite a few things that would have been seen as not merely bending the Mosaic rules but breaking them.

Besides these healings on the Sabbath, there was Jesus' willingness to say that "nothing that enters a person can make them unclean, but rather it is what comes out of a person's heart that makes them unclean" (Mark 7:5). The more you study the Jesus stories, the more you realize Jesus is not just a reformer of early Judaism, he really believes the end times have begun and with it the new covenant, which eclipses the various forms of the old covenant.

JESUS THE SAGE

One of the keys to understanding Jesus is recognizing that his main public form of discourse in Galilee—and also in Judaea, albeit in a different form—was wisdom speech. The Jesus of Mark's Gospel, in fact, tells us that Jesus determined that he would teach all things to those outside the circle of discipleship in *paraboloi*. But what in the world were "parables"?

While we are accustomed to think of parables as "an earthly story with a heavenly meaning," the Hebrew term *mashal*, like the Greek term *parabolos*, covers a lot more ground than just short fictional stories. Notice how, for example, the saying "physician heal thyself" is called a "parable" in Luke 4:23. This is just a metaphorical saying, not a story at all. Its best definition is that a *mashal/parabolos* is a metaphorical form of speech, which often involves analogy meant to tease the mind into active thought. A proverb, an aphorism, a riddle ("It is easier for a camel to crawl through the eye of a needle..."), a narrative parable, and even an allegory can be called a "parable." The term is shorthand for wise speech in metaphorical form, of whatever sort. Jesus' wisdom speech differed from many other Jewish teachers. His was about the inbreaking of God's final acts of redemption and judgment so that one day, "Thy Dominion come, thy will be done, on earth, as it is in heaven." It will be helpful to explore a small sampling of Jesus' wisdom speech at this juncture and speak briefly about his narrative thought world.[5]

Without question, Jesus is one of the great sages of all time and that includes being a great storyteller. Whether we consider his original parables or his creative handling of Old Testament stories, he is quite the improviser. He lived out of and spoke into a rich storied world, and he told his own and others' tales in light of the dawning end-time realities. Not surprisingly, his storied world is populated chiefly by Old Testament figures and events, alluded to, retold, and recycled in various ways, but also his storied world involves the spinning out of new tales, often in the form of parables or visionary remarks (for example, "I saw Satan fall like lightning from heaven," Luke 10:18). The function of Jesus' discourse was not merely to inform but also to transform, and that transformation was to involve not merely the audience's symbolic universe but also its behavior, in relationship to God as well as in relationship to one another. In other words, there was both a theological and an ethical thrust to Jesus' teaching. The stories were meant to transform not only the religious imagination of the audience but also their way of living, giving them samples and examples of how to believe and behave in the light of the in-breaking dominion of God.

If there is an essential difference in the way Jesus articulated his end-time worldview from that of his predecessor John the Baptizer, it is that Jesus, even in his more apocalyptic sayings, tended to emphasize the good news about the coming of the Dominion on earth. "The object of winnowing is not to collect enough chaff to have a glorious bonfire; it is to gather the wheat into the granary; the bonfire is purely incidental."[6] Thus, Jesus set about to rescue the perishing and to free Israel from its various forms of bondage. In this, Jesus is not trying to be Israel any more than the Twelve were set up initially to be Israel. All of them were trying to free Israel through a mission of preaching, teaching, and healing. There was, however, urgency and corporate focus to what they did. "The disciples were not evangelistic preachers sent out to save individual souls for some unearthly paradise. They were couriers proclaiming a national emergency and conducting a referendum on a question of national survival."[7] The storm of judgment was looming on the horizon for the Jewish faith centered on temple, territory, and Torah. God was intervening in Jesus and his followers before this disaster happened, just as he had already intervened through John the Baptizer. It is this context of social unrest and sense of impending doom that we must keep in view when considering the way Jesus articulates his thought world and the urgency with which he stresses certain things.

This line of discussion raises the issue of the relationship of Jesus to Israel. I suggest that Jesus presents himself not as Israel but rather as the Son of Man, and as the Son of Man, he is *Adam gone right*. That is, the scope of his messianic ministry is much broader than fulfilling the promise of being the ultimate Son of David, restoring Israel and its reign in the Holy Land. That is a part of what Jesus is about, but only a part. The temptation scenes make clear that something more wide-ranging and more cosmic is at stake, for Jesus is tempted as Son of God, not as Israel or Son of David. The issue is, what sort of Son of God was Jesus to be?

7

Was it one that comported with his being the true Son of Man of Danielic prophecy or not? Of course, Jesus spoke to a different audience than did his later Christian followers. Every single one of the New Testament documents is written for Christians, even if in some cases written for Christians to use in some form with outsiders. Jesus, on the other hand, was addressing Jews, even when he was addressing his disciples, and so he was able to presuppose the storied world of the Old Testament as something that he and his audience shared. This perhaps explains why Jesus is able to simply allude to figures such as the queen of the South (Matthew 12:41-42 and the parallels in Mark and Luke), or Noah (Matthew 24:36-41), or a widow in Zarephath (Luke 4:26) and expect the audience to know who he meant.

It is no surprise that many of the figures from the past of whom Jesus speaks are associated with judgments past and future, including both the queen of the South and Noah. According to Matthew 12:38-40 (cf. Matthew 16:1-4; Luke 11:29-32), the only "sign" that a wicked generation would get out of Jesus was the sign of Jonah, that reluctant crisis intervention specialist called upon to warn the people of Nineveh of impending disaster if they did not repent. Jonah 3:4 says that the Ninevites were warned that if they did not repent, destruction would fall upon them within forty days. Jesus offers a similar warning in Mark 13, except that the clock is set to forty years. Luke, in his relating of this sort of teaching, makes it all the more explicit that Jesus means the destruction of Jerusalem by human armies, namely, Roman armies (Luke 19:41-44; 21:20-24; 23:27-31).

It is interesting, however, that most of the stories that Jesus told were of his own making, stories about contemporaries and contemporary things, such as the coming of God's end-time saving activity. As we read through even just the narrative parables, we find anonymous human figures providing examples of various sorts. Only the parable of the rich man and Lazarus presents a story about a named individual (Luke16:19-31). Even more interesting is the fact that God is portrayed as an actor in various of these parables; he is the owner of the vineyard in the parable of the wicked tenants (Mark 12:1-11), and the forgiving Father in the parable of the prodigal son (Luke 15:11-32). Most important, we discover that Jesus provides an example of how to do theology and ethics in story form, for these stories are about both divine activity and human responses of various sorts.

There is also a dark edge to the stories that Jesus tells when it comes to the evaluation of his own people. By this I mean that they are portrayed as lost (see Luke 15) and their leaders as those who reject God's emissaries the prophets and even his Son (Matthew 23:29-39). The end-time situation is portrayed as drastic, with all sorts of unexpected persons trying to race through the narrow gate into the kingdom, while the invited guests have snubbed the host and either refused to come or have come late and without the appropriate attire. Pious Jews are going away from temple prayer unjustified while tax collectors are being accepted. There is some sort of drastic reversal of normal expectations happening as the Dominion breaks into human history, and it does not bode well for the faithful elder brothers of the family, it would appear. God is busy vindicating the oppressed, liberating the lost, enfranchising the least and last, and changing the guest list at the messianic banquet. These are stories about the upsetting of a highly stratified world, about the changing of the guard, about new occasions teaching new duties, about both judgment and redemption catching Jews by surprise, and perhaps most of all about the need for repentance by one and all as God's divine saving activity is happening in their midst, and yet many are blind to it.

The storied world that Jesus tells of has not only a dark edge but also a strangeness. Good shepherds do not normally leave ninety-nine sheep to rescue one straggler. People do not plant a weed such as a mustard bush, as it only attracts the wrong sort of birds and attention. God is not like an unjust judge who has to be forced into vindicating a persistent widow. We could go on. Jesus is offering new perspectives on old images and ideas and, in some cases, new perspectives on new vistas and horizons that are coming into view.

N. T. Wright rightly senses what is going on in Jesus' ministry when he says,

> The crucial element in his prophetic activity was the story, both implicit and explicit, that he was telling and acting out. It was Israel's story reaching its climax: the long-awaiting moment has arrived! ... To say 'the kingdom of God is at hand' makes sense only when the hearers know 'the story thus far' and are waiting for it to be completed.[8]

And precisely because Jesus is operating in the Jewish ethos of the land of Israel he can presuppose a storied world context that most of the writers of the New Testament cannot presuppose. This may well explain why we find no parables outside the Gospels. It is because we are no longer speaking into Jesus' specific world, a world where Jewish wisdom with an end-of-days twist made sense.

In its own context, then, how would Jesus' articulation of his vision in stories have been heard? Again Wright helps us: "It would clearly *both* challenge some prevailing assumptions within that Jewish context *and* retain a special focus which would be characteristic only of Jesus' career, not the work of his post-Easter followers. It must be set within Judaism, but as a challenge; it must be the presupposition for the church, but not the blueprint."[9] Just so, and this means that it is crucial to get the balance right between continuity and discontinuity when it comes to assessing the storied world of Jesus and of his post-Easter followers. And again, the point of the parables is to reorder the thinking of Jews: "The parables offer not only information, but challenge; they are stories designed to evoke fresh praxis, to reorder the symbolic world, to break open current understandings and inculcate fresh ones."[10]

A good example to examine closely is the parable of the sower in Mark 4:1-9. Here we have the revolutionary notion that Jesus is the person who is bringing the story of Israel to a climax in his own ministry. "If we fail to see how profoundly subversive, how almost suicidally dangerous, such a claim was," it is because we have tended to turn Jesus' counter-order wisdom speech into innocuous sermon illustrations.[11] It is right to say that when we are dealing with the narrative parables, we need to follow the narrative logic of the story, not assume that these are thinly veiled allegories of history in detail. At the same time, there are allegorical elements in Jesus' parables, and especially perhaps this one. Modern distinctions between parable and allegory are not all that helpful when it comes to ancient Jewish storytelling. Who, then, is the sower in this parable? Along with most commentators, I agree that it is Jesus, assuming a divine role here of planting God's Word about the dominion in surprising as well as familiar places.

There are some surprising results of following this narrative logic. For one thing, Jesus is not sanguine that most of those who hear him will respond positively in the long term. He is unlike the naive and overly optimistic preacher of today. But what is perhaps most telling about this parable is that Jesus expects rejection and ephemeral positive responses. He expects too much competition to allow his message to grow in the hearts of many. He expects absolute, hard-hearted rejection. And yes, in the good soil he expects good, long-lasting results.

This is an odd message for a person who saw himself in a messianic light, as one who had come to rescue Israel from disaster. In a sense, it is a message about the end of one thought world and the unexpected beginnings of another out of the ashes of the first one. In Jesus' view, his world is hell-bent, not heaven bound; and he, like John the Baptizer, has come to try to rescue a few of the perishing before the dark night of judgment falls. This parable differs considerably from the one in Mark 12:1-11 about the wicked tenants, as that is a commentary on Jewish leadership in the vineyard, not about the state of the Jewish vineyard in general. But both parables presuppose that things are coming to a climax, and that God's last-ditch efforts to rescue his people are culminating in the ministry of Jesus, who seeks to reclaim God's land, his vineyard, before it produces nothing but the grapes of wrath.

Along with Wright, I think that the aforementioned parables in Mark 4 and Mark 12 would have been seen as echoing or alluding to Isaiah 5–6. In this light, there can be no question but that the vineyard is Israel, and Jesus sees himself as fulfilling a prophetic role like that of Isaiah, dealing with hard-of-hearing Israel. But what is most telling when we closely read Isaiah 5–6 and then think of these two parables of Jesus is that already in Isaiah the theme of impending judgment and the exile of God's Jewish people is clear. In this context, the use of parables reflects and indeed presupposes the hard-heartedness of the audience and their refusal to listen. They will not hear and understand unless they turn or repent. Listen to some of Isaiah's Song of the Vineyard:

> What more could have been done for my vineyard
>> than I have done for it?
> When I looked for good grapes,
>> why did it yield only bad?
> Now I will tell you
>> what I am going to do to my vineyard:
> I will take away its hedge,
>> and it will be destroyed;
> I will break down its wall,
>> and it will be trampled. (Isaiah 5:4-5)

The song is a lament that goes on to bemoan the injustice and bloodshed in Israel.

Here is where I say that this all comports nicely with Jesus' prediction of the demise of the temple and Jerusalem in Mark 13. In Jesus' view, as his prophetic sign-act in the temple showed, this temple was the temple of doom, one that God would judge within a generation. And indeed, exactly one biblical generation (40 years) after Jesus died in A.D. 30 the temple fell in Jerusalem to the Romans. Jesus was no false prophet any more than Isaiah was in regard to the demise of Jerusalem and exile in his own era. In light of all this, it is interesting that the later Christian followers of Jesus not only continued to evangelize Jews and see God as promising them much but also, as a text such as Romans 11 shows, they continued to believe that God, though he might temporarily break off Jews from his people who did not accept Jesus as their messiah, would not replace an unresponsive Jewish people with a more responsive Gentile one. This is surprising only to those who do not know the regular pattern in the Old Testament prophetic oracles of redemption of Israel after and indeed as a result of judgment on Israel (see, for example, Hosea, Amos, and, of course, Isaiah). Perhaps most radically and paradoxically, Jesus was suggesting in Mark 4 that God's radical rescue of his people would come not by means of military action or a warrior-messiah but rather through the call of and response to Jesus' preaching of the good news.

This brings us to the other seed parables in Mark 4. Jesus seems to think that there will be some "seedy" characters, indeed some characters that Jews would consider "for the birds" (cf. Daniel 4:20-22) in the dominion, to the surprise of the long-time dwellers there. Hence, Jesus tells the parable of the mustard seed, a seed that no Jewish farmer would ever plant in a garden. The parable of the mustard seed is a parable of contrast between small beginnings and large, if noxious and surprising, outcomes; but it is also a parable that tells us what sort of persons were going to end up in the vineyard: the wild birds from afar, which should probably be seen as an allusion to Gentiles. The parable of the seed growing secretly tells us something about the method by which the Dominion is coming: secretly, under the radar, without a lot of human effort, and certainly without violence. This parable can be fruitfully compared to the parable of the leaven in the dough (Matthew 13:33; Luke 13:20-21) in that both suggest a sort of automatic process, one without human aid that produces the result. The hiddenness theme is also evident in parables of the pearl of great price and the treasure in the field (Matthew 13:44-46).

There are apocalyptic overtones to all these parables as they emerge from a world of opacity, of secrets that require teasing the brain into active thought to figure out, of God producing a crop and a harvest or a treasure as if by sleight of hand. The harvest theme is a dead giveaway that Jesus believed that the end-times scenario was already in play. And here precisely is where I differ strongly with Wright. These are not parables about return from exile. If anything, they are parables about the surprising presence of God's saving activity in the midst of occupation and oppression in the Holy Land, a very different message indeed. Jesus did not come to meet the audience's messianic expectations; he came to meet their needs. But ultimately, that task could be consummated only through a sacrifice on a cross and its sequel. Redemption would not come on the cheap or even just by a spiritual revival of good preaching accompanied by some miracles. The sin problem would not be dealt with or overcome by those means alone. And this brings us to another crucial point.

Did Jesus tell stories about himself? One could argue that Jesus appears in some of the parables. For example, in Mark 4 he seems to be the sower, and in Mark 12, it seems clear enough that he is the Son who is rejected, killed, and thrown out of the vineyard. We could perhaps also suggest that in the parable of the lost sheep, he is the shepherd, or in the parable of the lost coin, he is the woman seeking the coin (see Luke 15:3-10). But these parables in the main are not about the king Jesus; they are about the coming of the kingdom of God.

When Jesus referred to himself, he chose a phrase that we do not find in any of the parables: the "Son of Man." A close examination of his use of this term shows that at least a good bit of the time he is alluding to the story of that enigmatic "one like a son of man" in Daniel 7:13-14, the one who would be given a kingdom by God and would rule and judge the earth forever. This is especially clear in a saying such as that in Mark 14:62, but it is also in evidence in other Son of Man sayings, even in the Johannine tradition (see John 1:51; 3:13; 8:28). Jesus, it appears, exegeted his own career, purpose, existence, and importance out of various Old Testament stories, and I suggest that this influenced the various christological hymns that his earliest followers created after Easter. The link between the proclaimer and becoming the one proclaimed becomes clearer when we realize that Jesus also exegeted himself out of the Old Testament story of Wisdom (see Proverbs 8–9 and compare Wisdom of Solomon). This is especially clear in various places in Matthew 11, especially Matthew 11:19, where Jesus calls himself Wisdom directly. Then too we must point to a text such as Mark 12:35-37, where Jesus cleverly intimates in his interpretation of Psalm 110 that the messiah is in fact not just David's son, but even greater than that, he is David's lord; and in either case he is alluding to himself there. Jesus himself, then, provided the catalyst for interpreting and explaining his significance out of the prophetic and wisdom literature of early Judaism. We will say much more about this in the final chapter of this study.

Jesus is not merely telling a story or carrying a story already in play forward to its logical climax. This becomes quite clear in, for example, his "yoke" saying (Matthew 11:28-30), where it is Jesus' yoke that his disciples are to take upon themselves with rigor and vigor, not the yoke of the Mosaic law. The Mosaic law, having been fulfilled in the Christ event, would not provide the ethical script for all Christian conduct going forward; rather, the law of Christ would do so. Of course, this would be confusing because some elements of the Mosaic law would be renewed or reaffirmed or intensified by Christ—for example, the Great Commandment —and thus would be part of the binding contract known as the new covenant. But Christ's followers would do these things because they were part of Christ's yoke, which he commanded his disciples to take up, called, paradoxically, a light burden. They would not merely continue the story of obedience (and disobedience) of Israel to Moses' law.

However subversive or paradoxical the later Christian message may have seemed and however much they may have relied on Jesus' message, even his message about himself, Christian preachers did not by and large follow Jesus' methodology of preaching. They told the story straight. Partly, this had to do with ethos and social context, since most audiences outside Israel were not well-schooled in Jewish wisdom literature. However, this also partly had to do with the change in symbolic universe from before to after the death and resurrection of Jesus. The proclaimer had become the universally proclaimed, and this is because of the way his life turned out.

Apparently, it was felt that the message about a crucified and risen messiah was paradoxical enough in itself, and required enough explaining in itself, that an evangelistic religion needed to tell the story in a clear and straightforward way. While some of the themes of the "good news" song and part of the tune remained the same, the lyrics needed to be less enigmatic and more singularly focused on Jesus himself and his redemptive work.

It was the Frenchman Alfred Loisy who famously once said that Jesus preached the Kingdom, but it was the church that showed up. What Loisy did not really grasp, it would appear, is that what Jesus was preaching was the divine saving intervention of God through his own ministry and that of his disciples, and in this sense, it certainly did show up both during and after the life of the historical Jesus. Without the coming of the Son of Man there would have been no good news of the Kingdom, and without his death, resurrection, and return, there would have been no completion to the arc of the story Jesus believed he was living out of: the story in Daniel 7 of the one like a Son of Man who came down from heaven to rule forever on earth and to be worshiped by every tribe and tongue and people and nation. In Daniel 7, we see the harmonic converge in the key elements in Jesus' message—kingdom of God and Son of Man—and it was, and is, and ever shall be only the latter that brings the former on earth, as it is in heaven.

I would like to close with a story. Shelly Jackson, a gifted writer, has set out on a remarkable project to enflesh a story of hers, quite literally. The story has 2,095 words and is titled "Skin." She has asked for volunteers from all over the world to have exactly one word of the story tattooed on some readily visible part of their skin. She has not only had some takers, she has had more takers than she needs to tell this story in the flesh, to incarnate this story on living human beings.

What if the message of Jesus can be truly and fully understood only when it is set in the larger context of Jesus' own narrative thought world and when it is incarnated in us, *and only together as a living group can we make sense of it, with each one of us having but one piece of the puzzle to contribute to that understanding of the story?* What if the message of Jesus and the meaning of the Christ event can only be understood and believed when it is experienced and lived out in *koinonia*, in community, in love, in self-sacrifice, in service to others? I suspect that since Hurricane Katrina, those of you who live in New Orleans and have participated in the recovery efforts may well have gotten a glimpse of how true that is. We are not, or at least ought not to be, merely witnesses as the saints go marching in. Rather we have or should become part of "that number," part of the grand narrative, a story in which we become what we admire, we become like the one we emulate. And so when the story is lived out through us, we come to understand and believe in the Son of Man and his Kingdom, and so reflect his indelible image, renewed in us.

NOTES

1. Ben   Witherington III, *On the Road with Jesus: Birth and Ministry* (Nashville: Abingdon Press, 2011).

2. See Ben Witherington III, *Jesus the Seer* (Peabody, Mass.: Hendrickson, 1999).

3. Intertestamental Judaism existed between the times of the Old and New Testaments.

4. For a detailed study of this, see Bem Witherington III, *Jesus the Sage* (Minneapolis: Augsburg Fortress, 1994).

5. A extended treatment of this material that follows in the next paragraphs can be found in my *Indelible Image*, vol. 1 (Downer's Grove, Ill.: InterVarsity, 2009).

6. G. B. Caird, *New Testament Theology* (Oxford: Oxford University Press, 1994), 360.

7. Caird, 361.

8. N. T. Wright, Jesus and the Victory of God, vol. 2 of *Christian Origins and the Question of God* (Minneapolis: Fortress, 1996), 226.

9. Ibid.

10. Ibid., 229.

11. Ibid., 235.

CHAPTER TWO

JESUS' GREATEST HITS: THE SERMON ON THE MOUNT

*Matthew 5–7, perhaps more than any other portion of
the Gospels, has been dramatized, secularized, universal-
ized, criticized, psychologized, politicized and radicalized.*
—C. Bauman

Without question, the most discussed and debated portion of
Matthew's Gospel over the many centuries of Christian history is Matthew 5–7, the so-called Sermon on the Mount, though
it would be better called the teaching on the mount. Most scholars
see this material as a collection of important things Jesus said at various times in various ways in various locations, and thus it has come
to be viewed as a compendium—a sort of Jesus' Greatest Hits.
Scholars think this for two reasons: (1) this same material shows up
in various places in Luke's Gospel, and (2) the First Evangelist
clearly has a tendency to group together materials topically. Even a
moments' reflection on the other Gospels shows that Jesus didn't
spend one day just talking and the next day just healing, alternat-
ing back and forth. Yet this is the structure of Matthew's Gospel.
There is a block of teaching, followed by a block of narratives of
actions, repeated over and over again until we get to the Passion
narratives about the last week of Jesus' life. Whatever the composi-
tion history of Matthew 5–7, it will repay our close scrutiny.

GENERAL ORIENTATION TO MATTHEW 5-7

We have already remarked on Jesus being a sage—a wise man who taught in ways that characterize Jewish wisdom literature, such as parables, proverbs, aphorisms, riddles, and the like. This form of teaching led to the suggestion that Jesus was rather like Solomon, a famous writer and collector of proverbs, and Jesus himself suggests that he is not merely like King Solomon, he is Wisdom come in person, the very embodiment of the mind of God, hence "something greater than Solomon is here" as Jesus himself stressed.

But Jesus was not just any sort of sage or wise man, and this becomes clear even at the beginning of the Sermon on the Mount, which starts with the Beatitudes. The Beatitudes talk about blessings now and rewards later at the end of the age when the Kingdom fully comes on earth. Jesus' teaching, including his ethics, is a Kingdom ethic, by which I mean that it is based on the premise that God is currently intervening in human history to save his people—indeed to save everyone. Kingdom refers to the current and future divine saving activity and rule of God that goes on until God's will is fully done on earth as in heaven.

It needs to be stressed at the outset, that although Matthew tells us there was a crowd listening to Jesus' teaching, that teaching is primarily addressed to and directed to his disciples. These are not ethics for just anyone or chicken soup for any soul, these are marching orders for those prepared to follow Jesus. If you don't believe God's saving activity is happening in and through Jesus and are not a follower of Jesus, then all bets are off. Though many people over the ages, including non-Christians such as Gandhi, have drawn on this teaching and made it their own, this clearly is intended for followers of Jesus and anyone prepared to become such a follower.

There is a rhyme and reason, even a structure to this sermon. Jesus works through familiar standing topics that were a part of early Jewish wisdom—teachings on wealth, health, loyalties, marriage, divorce, adultery, singleness, and of course religious practices like prayer, fasting, and almsgiving. But it is not just teaching about actions, it's also about attitudes of the heart—anxiety, lust, a judgmental attitude, love, deceit, greed, pride, and much more. And it's also about speech patterns, about words, about controlling the tongue. So Jesus has something to say about calling people fools, speaking blasphemy, swearing oaths, and the like.

If we are looking for a structure to the material, what we find, as R. Guelich pointed out, are: (1) Blessings (5:3-16), which serve as an introduction to the discourse as a whole (We start with grace and move on to admonitions.); (2) the Greater Righteousness (5:17–7:12); and (3) the Alternatives (7:13-27).[1] We need to bear in mind several other factors. While there is something of a similarity between this material and Proverbs 1–6 or the early Jewish wisdom book called Sirach, neither of those two books present us with wisdom set in a Kingdom or end-time context. Furthermore, Jesus' wisdom is not merely wisdom deduced from a close reading of nature or human nature, as much of previous wisdom literature had been; he offers both revelatory wisdom (wisdom only God knows and must reveal) and counter order (even counterintuitive) wisdom. When we hear things like "the last shall be first and the first shall be last," we are not hearing common-sense wisdom. That is not the way of the world, but it is the way of the Kingdom where the least, the last, and the lost become the foremost, the first, and the found.

Finally, it is worth pointing out that Jesus is not simply reiterating the Torah, the Law of Moses, here. He talks about the Law and the Prophets being fulfilled. How do we make sense of this? Is Jesus just giving us the Amplified Version of Mosaic Law here? The answer to this is no. For one thing, we do not simply have apodictic statements here, laws. We have beatitudes, parables, admonitions, exhortations, and a variety of other things. But we ought not to contrast Gospel and Law, for Gospel includes commandments as the Sermon on the Mount shows. However, the subject of the Sermon on the Mount is not, What must I do to be born again? This is teaching for those who are already disciples of Jesus or are ready to take on that challenge. It would be more correct to say, "This is teaching on how to become more Christlike and do a better job of being his disciple."

Jesus inaugurated a new covenant; he did not simply restate or reinforce an old one such as the Mosaic covenant. He included in the commandments and teachings of the new covenant something old, something new, something borrowed, and something true. Sometimes Jesus reiterates Old Testament teaching. Sometimes he intensifies Old Testament teaching. Sometimes he offers new teaching such as "no oaths at all" or no retaliation of any kind or love even your enemies and pray for those who persecute you. When Jesus says he came to fulfill the Law and the Prophets, the word fulfill is end-time language, language that indicates something is coming to completion, to an end. Jesus, in his life, fulfilled the Law and the Prophets on behalf of God's people, fulfilling all righteousness, so to speak, even paying the price for the people's sins by offering himself as an atoning sacrifice on the cross. So one covenant is coming to a close—to fulfillment in the life, death, and resurrection of Jesus—and another is being born. Jesus' ministry is the time of the overlap of the two, for the Kingdom is already and not yet. This is why, on the one hand, Jesus can exhort the Pharisees to go on tithing dill, mint, and cumin without neglecting the weightier matters of the Law; but he can say to his own disciples that new occasions teach new duties, that the end-time Kingdom has some different rules—for example it does not require the keeping of the food laws (see Mark 7, especially the parenthetical comment at Mark 7:19).

In a dramatic gesture, Jesus presents himself as the Wisdom of God come in person that eclipses the Mosaic wisdom; and he says, "Come unto me all you who are heavy laden and I will give you rest. Take my yoke upon you, and learn from me, for my yoke is easy, and my burden is light" (Matthew 11:28-30). What most people do not realize is that this is almost a direct quote from Sirach, but in Sirach 6:26-30, the yoke being referred to is the Old Testament Wisdom of God (see also Sirach 51:26). In Matthew, however, Jesus presents himself as the yoke-giver and the teacher of wisdom and commandments and, indeed, the earthly embodiment of the wisdom and will of God. Bearing these things in mind, we can look at the sermon in some detail, starting with the Beatitudes.

THE BEATITUDES

These beautiful but paradoxical words (Why in the world should those mourning be seen as blessed?) are some of the most familiar in all the Gospels. But when one goes to the hill that overlooks the Sea of Galilee, to the beautiful garden where pilgrims come to "the Mount of Beatitude," it is easy to overspiritualize these blessings and miss their edginess. It is not true in the ordinary course of human affairs that the merciful receive mercy, nor do all those who mourn get comforted. What these Beatitudes presuppose, however, is that there is a God who blesses and who, through Jesus, is in the process of righting all wrongs and making things turn out well in the end. The point is, the person who believes and embraces this end-time perspective has found the source of true contentment or blessedness. In each case, with each beatitude, we are not dealing with general truisms for all naive or optimistic souls. In each case, we discover that being satisfied, obtaining mercy, being called children of God, and seeing God all refer to the destiny set aside for the disciples of Jesus, and not just for anyone under any circumstances. Indeed, what is envisioned is that these things will only fully come true in the end when faith turns to sight, and hope is realized, and love is all in all. These are not rules, or the "be happy" attitudes, for any and all lives or just any stage in human history. They do not work on the stage of human history apart from a context of Christ's work and the destiny of his followers. For them, the future is as bright as the promises and blessings of God.

The context of all this is the action of God that both precedes and rewards the faithful response of the disciple. The focus here is not only on actions but also on some attitudes. We need, of course, to realize that this is but a sampling of the beatitudes we find in the Gospels—there are twenty-eight just in Matthew and Luke, and seven in Revelation, for example.

The eight Beatitudes are very carefully arranged, with the first and last involving present-tense verbs and the middle ones all having future verbs. Only the last of these is in the second person and more direct ("blessed are you..."). A comparison with Old Testament beatitudes suggests that where Matthew and Luke both present us with a form of the same beatitude (for example, "Blessed are the poor in spirit" [Matthew] as compared to "Blessed are the poor" [Luke]), the Matthean form is more likely to be original. Many scholars note the similarity between the first and third beatitudes, but in any case it is clear that Jesus believed the dominion of God had already begun to be realized on earth through his ministry. I would suggest that Matthew has arranged these beatitudes to show the fulfillment of Isaiah 61:1-3. Jesus also draws on this passage in his inaugural synagogue sermon in Nazareth (see Luke 4):

> The Spirit of the Sovereign LORD is on me,
>> because the LORD has anointed me
>> to preach good news to the poor.
> He has sent me to bind up the brokenhearted,
>> to proclaim freedom for the captives
>> and release from darkness for the prisoners,
> to proclaim the year of the LORD's favor
>> and the day of vengeance of our God,
> to comfort all who mourn,
>> and provide for those who grieve in Zion—
> to bestow on them a crown of beauty
>> instead of ashes,
> the oil of gladness
>> instead of mourning,
> and a garment of praise
>> instead of a spirit of despair.
> They will be called oaks of righteousness,
>> a planting of the LORD
>> for the display of his splendor.

Now what is interesting about this likely Old Testament background to the Beatitudes in Matthew 5 is that it implies that Jesus sees himself as the Servant of the LORD who is speaking in Isaiah 61. But what does it mean to talk about the poor in Spirit? It is unlikely, in light of the Isaiah 61 background, that Jesus referred to either (1) a spiritualized physical poverty or (2) persons who lack the Holy Spirit. No, Jesus is talking about the depressed oppressed. That is, he is talking about those who are low in spirits due to abuse and oppression. Such people recognize their need for God and turn to God. The main stress would be on their social condition but with an allusion to their attitude. The point is not to single out spiritually deficient disciples as opposed to those who aren't. The persons in mind are in a social condition that makes them acutely aware of their frailty and need for God.

The second beatitude speaks not of those who have just lost a loved one but of those who are disenfranchised, overcome with their lostness or helplessness in a hostile world because of their allegiance to God. The third beatitude refers to the gentle, with a reminder that the meek are not the weak. They will inherit the earth. One of my favorite *Far Side* cartoons shows a meek and mild-mannered man sitting at a desk across from his accountant. The caption says "The day after the meek inherit the earth," and the accountant is saying to the man, "What we have here is a pretty serious capital gains problem." What meekness actually refers to is not an attitude but rather total dependency on God. The beatitude about the merciful indicates that they will be treated at the final judgment as they have treated others. Verse 8 stresses that without personal holiness, no one can enter into the holy presence of God. Jesus doesn't indicate here how one obtains the condition of purity of heart, but he does see it as a necessary condition. Jesus does not say, "Blessed are those who know I am holy and righteous and pure on their behalf." He says those actually pure in heart will see God. Verse 9 speaks of those actively pursuing peace and reconciliation between peoples. They establish shalom and well-being between peoples. Verse 10 talks about suffering for righteousness' sake, which presumably means for the Kingdom and its principles and, indeed, for Jesus' sake. Notice in all these beatitudes, neither heaven nor the end-time Kingdom is said to be a reward for such behavior. Rather, there are rewards "in heaven" and "in the Kingdom."

The theme of the character of a disciple is announced in the Beatitudes, but it is dealt with in more depth in 5:13-16. Whereas in verses 11-12 we had the negative description of the cost of the discipleship, in verses 13-16, we have the positive description and responsibilities listed. What we need to know is that the term *salt* in wisdom literature refers to "wisdom," hence the verb that suggests the opposite of having salt in oneself means being foolish. There is probably a play on words here in the Aramaic—for *tabel* and *tapel* mean, respectively, "salt" and "foolish." The point is that if a disciple ceases to function in the one capacity in which he is truly valuable, namely witnessing to the world by word and deed, then that disciple is worthless, fit only to be cast out (noting the end-time judgment overtones here). The second metaphor indicates that a disciple who does his job in a fallen and wicked world will stand out like a sore thumb, like a city set on a hill. We are called to be a light to the world rather than curse the world's darkness. There is an implicit universalism here: we are not merely to be a light to God's people but to a dark world. Of course if you illuminate those who are in darkness, they may either see the light or curse it for blinding them.

LAYING DOWN THE LAW

Matthew 5:17-20 is one of the more familiar sections of this sermon and one of the most debated. Verse 17 should be compared to Matthew 10:34, which has the same form. Our verse is meant to deny that Jesus came to do something negative—to annul or set aside the Law and the Prophets, a shorthand way of referring to the whole of the Hebrew Scriptures. Instead of that, he came to fulfill them. Notice it does not say he came to reaffirm them or to declare them eternally valid or the like. No, he personally came to fulfill both the Law and the Prophets. This is about part of his christological mission.

Jesus brings them both to their intended end or goal, bringing them to full fruition. He is the reality and his action, the culmination of what the Law and the Prophets were pointing to. Jesus was not abolishing the Law in the sense of declaring it untrue, but he was, by fulfilling it and proclaiming Kingdom come, indicating that it was no longer applicable carte blanche, but only insofar as and to the extent that Jesus reaffirmed it and reapplied it. None of the Law would be erased or abolished before it was all fulfilled and completed. The fulfilled portions no longer act as a norm. A truth does not become less true because it is a timely truth rather than a timeless one. The issue is how long and to whom is the Law applicable. Thus, Jesus makes very clear that there can be no antinomianism, no allergic reaction to law itself, among his followers. Indeed, Jesus will intensify some of the commandments and formulate additional, even more demanding ones. Strictly speaking, Gospel and Law are not mutually exclusive, for Gospel includes commandments. A high standard of righteousness is necessary if one is to enter the Dominion when it fully comes on earth.

The lengthy section Matthew 5:21-48 is bound together by the famous antitheses—"you have heard it said...But I say to you..." (verses 21, 27, 31, 33, 38, and 43). Jesus believed that the end-time situation was already in play. In these antitheses, there is some reaffirmation and amplification of existing Mosaic law, but that is not the whole story. For one thing, Jesus suggests that concession to sin (for example, the hardness of heart) such as those found in the Mosaic laws about divorce are abrogated in light of the new situation. God's original creation intentions for marriage, not the interim arrangements in the Mosaic law, now apply to marriage and singleness and divorce. Jesus in fact prohibits what Moses allows—divorce and oaths and murder, for example—and furthermore, Jesus allows what Moses prohibits— work on the Sabbath, fraternizing with unclean foreigners. And of course he places demands on his disciples in terms of sexual ethics (no lust in the heart) that go well beyond Mosaic strictures.

What comes across in this material is Jesus' sovereign freedom in the way he handles the law. Two guiding assumptions of Jesus explain this: the end-time situation is at hand and new occasions teach new duties. He himself is the bringer in not just of the Kingdom but also the new end-time covenant or contract between God and his people. Strictly speaking, from Jesus' point of view, one cannot violate or break a law that is obsolete or no longer in force. So, although Jesus would have appeared to be a lawbreaker to some of his Jewish contemporaries in various ways, doubtless he would and did dispute this view. Of course it was bound to be confusing that the new covenant did recycle some of the commandments from the old ones.

ATTITUDES AND ACTIONS TO AVOID

Six different topics are addressed in Matthew 5:21-46—anger, lust, divorce, oaths, revenge, and love. The first six verses deal with anger. Jesus' opening salvo recites Moses's prohibition against murder, but only as a taking-off point to discuss anger management. This means he is dealing with one of the root causes of murder and calling his disciples to deal with those root causes of sinful actions. He calls them to a higher standard of righteousness than Moses, including righteousness of thought, attitude, word, and deed. Notice that the term "brother" keeps coming up in this passage, indicating that indeed this is an ethic for disciples, not a utopian ethic meant to be imposed on society in general. We see an anger action cycle referred to here—first he refers to being angry, then he refers to angry actions such as calling people names (*raka* is an Aramaic term meaning "you fool"). And notice the escalation of possible punishments as things go from bad to worse: subject to judgment becomes answerable to the council becomes in danger of hellfire. We do need to bear in mind that wisdom language was often hyperbolic to make a strong point, but we should not overlook that Jesus is in earnest and dead serious about what he is saying here. He is not merely suggesting, "If it's not too much trouble, you might want to avoid these sorts of attitudes and actions." Jesus appears to be referring not just to any kind of anger but anger involving verbal abuse directed toward fellow believers. He is not, for example, talking about righteous anger in regard to sin or wrong done, something he himself exhibited from time to time without censuring or censoring himself (see Mark 1:41; 2:5; Matthew 21:12-17)! So he is talking about inappropriate anger and its inappropriate expression. It is possible that the story of Cain lies in the background here, a story about anger against a brother that leads to murder. Notice here and in Genesis 4 there is also the matter of sacrifice mentioned. Rage and wrathful actions including revenge are being prohibited here.

Verses 23-26 then provide practical advice on what to do if a believer has something against you. You should settle it before it goes to court with horrific consequences. Interestingly, this is advice on how to deal with another person's anger rather than how to stifle one's own. The point is to help believers live in community and communion with one another. Go and make it right, says Jesus, before you engage in acts of piety or charity. In Jesus' day there were debtors' prisons, and this seems to be the scenario he envisions—one person is angry because he is owed money or goods and is going to court to send the debtor to prison in retaliation for nonpayment. It is not an accident that one of the petitions of the Lord's Prayer is forgive us our debts as we forgive those indebted to us. When Jesus comes, a Jubilee including forgiveness of debts is proclaimed.

Matthew 5:27-32 is perhaps too familiar in an age that has such problems with Jesus' teaching on marriage, divorce, and adultery. All too often, however, familiarity leads to assuming that one understands the text when that may not be the case. The subject here is *moicheuo*, which normally refers to a very specific sexual sin of extramarital intercourse by a married person with someone betrothed or married who is not their spouse. In other words, adultery is in view here. It appears that in verses 27 and 32, the term is used of the act of adultery, but in verse 28, it is used more broadly. Verse 28 is often mistranslated and should probably be rendered, "he who so looks on a woman that she becomes desirous has already led her astray into adultery in his heart." This advice then targets male lust in the heart as the instigating cause of this sinful situation, which is strikingly different from the usual lament in early Judaism and in Greco-Roman literature about women being temptresses and thus the source of the problem. Jesus is protecting the more vulnerable member of society and holding the man responsible for upholding the community ethic in this matter. Male lust and male aggression, not male instability, is being critiqued.

Matthew 5:29-30 is entirely consistent with this rendering of verse 28. Jesus dramatically tells men who are unable to control themselves that they would be better to dismember themselves than to behave in ways that would send them to Gehenna. When he says, "If your eye causes you to sin, pluck it out, if your hand causes you to sin, cut it off," he is in fact talking about known punishments for things like voyeurism or stealing another's wife. The whole passage could be read not as hyperbole to make a point, but as a dramatic warning drawing on known punishments in the Holy Land.

In verses 31-32, we definitely have a dramatic contrast between the teaching of Moses and the teaching of Jesus. It seems clear that we should not simply equate the Greek term *porneia* (from which we get *pornography*) with the earlier term *moicheia*, which refers to adultery. A *porne* in antiquity was a prostitute, so the term *porneia* could refer to prostitution or frequenting prostitutes. The exception clause then could allow for divorce in the case of a wife who takes up prostitution. But *porneia*, when it is a technical term, can also refer to a different specific sexual sin, namely incest, a meaning it has in 1 Corinthians 5:1-2. In either case, it is unwise to translate the term as marital infidelity much less as adultery since a very different word has been used already in this chapter for adultery.

This brings us to an important point. Speaking to the disciples in Matthew 19, Jesus also offers this same teaching, and they react as if Jesus were severely restricting his male followers' abilities to divorce. One of them says, for example, "If this is the way it is between a man and a woman, it is better not to marry." This response only makes sense if Jesus' teaching is stricter than that of Moses; and indeed in 1 Corinthians 7, Paul tells us that Jesus' basic teaching was no divorce. The exception clauses then must refer to some sort of very exceptional situation, such as the incestuous marriage between Antipas and his brother's wife or the relationship referred to in 1 Corinthians 5. What Jesus would be saying in Matthew 5 and 19 is then "no divorce except when one has entered into an incestuous relationship, which is not a proper marriage to begin with, not a relationship where God had joined two people together." If the disciples cannot handle this strict prohibition of divorce, then Jesus says they can remain single for the sake of the Kingdom (Matthew 19:10-12, he uses the dramatic term *eunuch* to indicate complete celibacy in singleness).

A couple of more points should be stressed about this end-time teaching. Jesus defines marriage as a relationship in which God joins together one man and one woman. Heterosexual monogamy was his definition of marriage, not a broader or different definition. Entirely consistent with this is the only alternative he offers, namely, celibacy in singleness ("being a eunuch for the sake of the Kingdom"). Now, everyone in antiquity knew about eunuchs. They had had their genitals cut off, rendering them incapable of sexual activity. While it is doubtful that Jesus is counseling literally becoming a eunuch, it is clear that he means no sexual activity outside of marriage—whether heterosexual activity or homosexual activity. Sometimes it is suggested that Jesus has nothing to say about the current homosexual debate, but this is not so. He calls all those not engaged in heterosexual monogamy, whether gay or straight, to strict celibacy— no sexual relationships at all, whether of the premarital, extramarital, or homosexual variety.

In Matthew 5:33-37, the subject changes to oaths, which are permitted in Mosaic law provided they are not false or irreverent ones (Exodus 20:7; Leviticus 19:12; Numbers 30:3-15; Deuteronomy 23:21-23; compare Psalms 50:14b, which may be echoed in Jesus' teaching here). It is worth noting that Jesus simply says, "no oaths of any kind"—period. And in Matthew 26:53 we see him refusing to speak under oath. Of course the whole point of an oath is to vouch for the truthfulness of what one is saying or claiming. But Jesus is calling for such a high standard of integrity that one never needs to back up a statement or claim with an oath. He is requiring all disciples to be persons of their word, so that their yes means yes, and their no means no. The reference to yes and no suggests that Jesus mainly has promissory oaths in mind (that is, where one promises under oath to do something). Oath-taking changes nothing about the truth at all, and verse 37 even goes so far as to say that anything beyond a yes or a no comes from the Evil One because it is a form of exaggeration.

NON-RETALIATION AND LOVE

Matthew 5:38-42 makes clear that Jesus is calling his disciples to do what they ought to do, not merely what was legal to do or even what was thought of as justified retaliation on the basis of the *lex talionis* in the Old Testament (the law of "eye for eye and tooth for tooth," compare Exodus 21:24; Deuteronomy 19:21; Leviticus 24:20). The *lex talionis* had as its intent an attempt to limit revenge to a fitting and proportional response. But Jesus will set his own ethical agenda here.

On his own authority ("but I *say* to you") Jesus insists that his followers are not to respond in kind when harmed, they are to respond in kindness. The slap with the back of the hand on the right cheek was an attempt at shaming someone. It was an insult. Disciples are not to respond in kind and start a reciprocity cycle of ever-escalating reprisals. Luke 6:29 turns this into a response to violence in general, not just to an insulting slap in the face. Jesus then advises taking no legal action against someone who does this sort of thing to you. Verse 40 then deals with the opposite scenario when someone takes you to court. The advice here is that if they want some piece of clothing from you, just give it to them before they sue. This advice stands in striking contrast to that in Exodus 22:25-26; Deuteronomy 24:12-13.

The fundamental ethic of Jesus is the ethic of love, not of reciprocity ("Do unto others, as they have done for you"), indeed it is an ethic of proactive love rather than reactive reprisals. One is to do good to the neighbor and even to the pagan soldier who requires you to carry some burden or undertake some task whether you want to do it or not. The advice involves going beyond expected or required help. Generosity and kindness are to be shown to the beggar with no thought of return and without calculation. One gives simply because that is the characteristic of one's Master, and the disciples are to imitate his behavior. Self-sacrifice replaces enlightened self-interest or reciprocity.

The famous teaching about love of enemy is found at Matthew 5:43-48. This passage concludes the antithesis section and to some extent sums it up. Some of Jesus' teaching is not merely countercultural wisdom, it would have been seen as counterintuitive as well. What sense does it make to love those who hate and kill you? Verse 43 begins with a partial quote from the love command in Leviticus 19:18. Loving neighbors is one thing; loving enemies, however, is another. While the phrase "hate your enemies" is not found in the Old Testament or in rabbinic literature, we do find it among the Dead Sea Scrolls in a scroll known as "The Community Rule." Here the suggestion is that one should love the sons of light and hate the sons of darkness. This saying is not characteristic of early Jewish thinking at its highest and best. Notice, however, that Jesus is calling not merely for love of enemies but for prayer for them as well.

The enemy is further defined in verse 44b as a persecutor. It is not natural to love such a person or pray for them, but it is what Jesus called his disciples to do. He is urging conduct not conditioned by kinship or even commonsense reasoning or what might seem natural. Rather, the rationale for doing this is that God the Father loves even our enemies and blesses them with sunshine and rain as he does his own chosen people. Verse 46 would be seen as an offensive comparison. Who wants to be compared to a tax collector or to be said to behave like them? A comparison is being made between Jesus' followers and two of the least favorite groups of early Jews: tax collectors and pagans. For a Jew to be told he was no better than one of these two groups would be patently offensive. Self-serving in-group love is not what Jesus calls his followers to. Verse 48 should not be isolated from the rest of this passage; to be perfect as God is perfect is to love as God loves, and that includes loving one's enemies and persecutors. The reference here is to love in action, not to some moral condition called perfection. "The emphasis here is not on flawless moral character, but on whole-hearted devotion to the imitation of God, not in the perfection of his being but of his ways."[2] Of course this exhortation presupposes the previous work of God in the disciple's life, but notice that this exhortation is given to all the disciples. It is not just a council of perfection for the elite disciples. Here it might be worth remembering the words of Augustine: "give what you command LORD, and then command whatever you will." John Wesley put it this way: "God's commands are covered promises. When the text says 'Thou shalt love your enemy' it means not merely that you ought to do so, but that by God's grace you can and will do so."

PRAYER, FASTING, ALMSGIVING, JUDGING

The materials in Matthew 6–7 on prayer, fasting, almsgiving, judging, and the like address very traditional standing topics in early Jewish ethical discussion, for prayer, fasting, and almsgiving were at the heart of the piety of early Jews. Jesus, however, addresses these topics in his own special and distinctive ways. In Matthew 6:4 Jesus suggests that when it comes to prayer, we should be playing only to an audience of one—God. In an honor-and-shame culture, the temptation was to pray ostentatious prayers in public so one could garner praise from one's fellow devotees. But Jesus says the focus should be on doing righteousness and being devout, not on merely appearing to be so. They should not be doing things "in order to be seen" and so improve their honor rating in an honor-and-shame culture.

The saying about "the left hand" is interesting precisely because it was never the favored hand in these ancient cultures. Doing something with the left hand was less likely to bring praise and attention to oneself. The point is to act without self-consciousness, without calculation. Although a Greek word, *hypocrites*, from which we get the English word *hypocrite*, is certainly a word Jesus could have heard and known. A *hypocrites* was an actor in a play, and near Nazareth in Sepphoris, there was a theater where one could find such people. Jesus of course is using the term in a metaphorical way to critique those who appear to be something that they are not. Indeed, the term is never used literally or in a positive way in the Gospels.

In Matthew 6:5-15 we find the all too familiar Lord's Prayer, which should really be called the "disciple's prayer," since it is given by Jesus to his disciples as a blueprint for praying. It may of course also reflect Jesus' own prayer pattern, to judge from the praying we see Jesus doing in Gethsemane, where we hear about him addressing God as Abba, and saying "thy will be done" and "let this cup pass" (Mark 14:36 and the parallels in Matthew and Luke). It should be noted from the outset that we have a different and shorter form of this same prayer in Luke 11.

I suspect that Luke 11:1-2 gives us a clue as to the original setting of this teaching—the disciples ask Jesus to teach them the proper way to pray, just as John the Baptizer had taught his own disciples to pray. What they seem to be asking is for Jesus to teach them a distinctive way to pray that reflects his belief system and how he would want his followers to approach prayer. I would stress that this is a prayer for all disciples of Jesus to use. It is not intended as a prayer for all and sundry to use regardless of whether they follow Jesus or not. The phrase "pray in this fashion" suggests this is just a bare outline, not a detailing of all the things one should pray about and pray for. This once again is an example of Jesus' wisdom, but it is wisdom with one eye on the horizon and God's bringing in of the Kingdom on earth as it is in heaven.

In Matthew's presentation we first are given examples of how not to pray, followed by the beguilingly simple Lord's Prayer. Notice the contrast between public and private praying, praying with an audience and without. Prayer in early Judaism tended to be done at certain hours of the day. The prayer of a disciple is supposed to be a personal matter, not a public performance, and clearly a private venue for a private prayer is seen as most appropriate. This, however, should not be taken as a polemic against all forms of public or corporate or even formulaic praying. Indeed, the Lord's Prayer is a formulaic prayer. The point is to pray without attempting to show off to others. The reference to the "closet" is probably to the windowless small room in the middle of an early Jewish home, which was the only room with a door with a latch because it was the storeroom for dried goods and supplies.

Jesus believes public prayer is not necessary to get God's attention, and indeed prayer is not about informing God about things he might be otherwise unaware of! Nor does it mainly function to make other human beings aware of certain needs and situations. What verse 6c says is that our Father who sees in secret will "restore it to you." This suggests a situation where one has been wronged, and God rectifies the matter. God will make it worth the time and effort to pray.

Much has rightly been made about Jesus instructing his disciples to pray to "Abba," the Aramaic term of intimacy for "Father." It is not a slang term (for example, not "Daddy") but a term of intimacy a child would use with a beloved parent—"dear Father" would be close in English. To this day, there is no evidence in earlier Judaism of someone instructing Jews to pray to God as Abba, but it is true that the use of Father language in general was more prevalent in later Jewish wisdom literature than in the Old Testament itself. Jesus is indeed suggesting that his disciples can share in the intimacy of relationship with God that he himself has, for he addresses God as Abba (Mark 14:36). And we discover in a text such as Romans 8:15 that the church, including even Gentiles, continued to address God as Abba.

In verse 7 another negative example is set forth, and babbling or prattling like a child is probably being critiqued here, perhaps droning on and on reciting the same words or names for God is in view. Verbosity is critiqued here in contrast to the compactness of the Lord's Prayer. Pagans were noted for praying by using all sorts of words and names for deities just to cover all their bases, since they believed there were myriad gods, and they were unsure who was blighting them or blessing them. They sometimes even thought gods needed to be informed about things, but Jesus says the real God is not like that. He knows before we speak or act just exactly what we need. In Matthew it is clear that the Lord's Prayer is a corporate prayer as the address is "our Father" whereas in Luke it is just Abba/Father. While Luke's version is likely closer to the original length of the prayer, Matthew's seems closer to its original Jewish form and spirit (for example the word "debts" in Matthew as opposed to "trespasses" in Luke, which is a broader term).

The basic structure of the prayer in Matthew involves an opening invocation, three "thou" petitions, followed by three "we" petitions. The Matthean form is flavored more to the end times than the Lukan form and is likely closer to the original in this regard, although the phrases "who art in heaven" and "as in heaven so on earth" and possibly "but rescue us from the Evil One" are clarifying additions. Verses 14-15 are an expansion on the point made in verse 12. We should notice from the start the contrast between what is the case in heaven in regard to God's will and what is the case on earth. Indeed, it is precisely because of this disparity that prayer is necessary. God's will is ever so often not being done on earth.

In regard to the "thou" petitions, it can be asked, Who is supposed to be doing this hallowing, or doing his will, and when? Are verses 9-10 prayers that God's name will one day be hallowed and his will one day will be done on earth as in heaven? Or is this about God hallowing his own name and doing his own will? Is God both the subject and object of these petitions? Probably not in light of the end-time flavor of this whole discourse and Jesus' teaching in general. The pray-er is looking forward to the day when God's name will be properly hallowed and his will fully be done on earth as it is in heaven, and he is asking that that day come (compare, for example, Philippians 2:5-11, which speaks of the day when everyone will confess Jesus is Lord to the glory of God the Father). The prayer then emphasizes that Jesus and the disciple both realize that the Kingdom has not yet fully come on earth.

Verse 11 has been much debated. Does it mean give us today the bread for tomorrow or does it refer to daily bread? Either way it is a request for basic sustenance in life, not for abundance. Bread was the basic staple of the Ancient Near Eastern diet. The prayer suggests a person living hand to mouth, who needs to pray for bread every day. It also suggests daily dependence on God regardless of your abundance of food or lack thereof.

The second "we" petition reminds us that there is a clear connection between forgiving others and being forgiven by God. A person who refuses to forgive should not expect to be forgiven when the Dominion comes on earth. And a person who realizes she is forgiven should then apply the same mercy to others who need one's forgiveness. The parable of the unmerciful servant (when it came to debts) in Matthew 18 is a fuller illustration of this very point. An unforgiving Christian is an oxymoron, and he or she puts an impediment in the way of receiving final forgiveness from God. Jesus once more affirms that the behavior of the disciple after he becomes a follower of Jesus will indeed affect one's final status in the Kingdom. Verses 14-15 are not then comments on initial forgiveness at the point of being saved but rather final forgiveness, as the phrase "your heavenly Father will not forgive" suggests.

Verse 13 is also controversial. The noun *peirasmon* can mean either "temptation" or "testing" with the context determining the issue. James 1 of course says that God tempts no one. So since this is addressed to God it would be better rendered, "do not put us to the test." A test is something God can and does give (see Job 1–2) to strengthen one's character. But a temptation that the devil brings is intended to destroy one's character. The paradox is that what God intends as a test, the devil can use as a temptation as well.

There is an old Jewish wisdom prayer that this line may be modeled on: "do not bring me into the power of a sin, a tempta-tion, a shame." In any case, God is not viewed as the tempter in this petition in the prayer. The prayer involves asking for protec-tion from entering into the situation of a temptation, and so the following petition should likely be rendered "but deliver us from the Evil One"—not evil in the abstract but rather the personal incarnation of evil: Satan. Turning evil into a mere power or malignant force is a modern preoccupation. Early Jewish follow-ers clearly believed in a personal devil and in demons as well (compare Matthew 5:37 and 13:19).

It was Jesus who fed the hungry, liberated the demon-possessed, offered forgiveness of sins, enacted this prayer on earth in his ministry, and did God's will on earth. Here is a prayer we know God wishes to answer with a large YES! This prayer sug-gests that if we have our priorities straight we will pray first and foremost for the plan of God and his glory to be manifest on earth before we ask for personal help, even the basic necessities of life—bread and forgiveness and deliverance from evil. This prayer is about the basic physical and spiritual necessities of all human beings. And using this prayer as a blueprint, we can always ask—does my prayer measure up to the priorities of this model? Is my prayer something Jesus would sign his name to, judging on the basis of this prayer? After all, saying "in Jesus' name" at the end of a prayer is signing Jesus' name to the prayer.

The complaint about fasting in Matthew 6:16-18 is much the same as the complaint about praying in public to get attention. Jesus has a problem with using acts of piety to draw attention to oneself and to garner praise for oneself. Jesus says of such a per-son they already have their full reward. Here Jesus is talking about voluntary fasting, not a required fast (compare Luke 18:1). Notice there is no mention of a prescribed fast connected with some religious rite (a Nazaritic vow) or some Jewish festival. Surprisingly, this is the sole place in the New Testament where fasting is taught or encouraged, which is something of a shock when we consider how much later monastic and ascetical Christianity stressed it. Notice that Jesus says that when his disciples fast they should appear perfectly normal—face washed, head anointed. This stands in contrast to 2 Samuel 12:20 and Sirach 9:8, which suggest such acts of grooming were forbidden on a day of fasting. Those who pray and fast are not to make a show of appearing to be distressed or miserable. Rather, Jesus believes he and his followers are in an end-time situation that calls for joy. If they are thinking of rewards, then they should look only to the praise they get from God for such acts of piety.

The remainder of the material in the Sermon on the Mount seems to be arranged according to the petitions in the Lord's Prayer. By this I mean Matthew 6:19-24 serves as an amplification of the first three petitions in the prayer, whereas 6:25-34 parallels the daily bread petition. Matthew 7:1-5 expands on the forgiveness petition, and 7:6-11 parallels the two sayings in 6:13. Matthew 6–7 is not a random collection of Jesus' sayings.

Matthew 6:19-24 is about singleness of purpose—one's treasure, eye, and master indicate one's priorities in life. Verse 19 literally reads "Do not treasure up treasure on earth where moth and eaters can consume, and thieves can dig through [the house or treasury wall] and steal. Rather treasure up treasure in heaven where these things cannot happen." Lest we think this is merely about spiritual matters, verse 21 brings us to the point: where your treasure is, there will your heart be also. The heart in Semitic thinking was the control-center of the person—the center not just of feelings, but of thought and will and conscience as well. This little parable is insisting that whatever one values the most will determine one's life orientation—how one arranges one's acts and plans and living. One's treasure can be said to be the ultimate expression of one's person and personality. The point is not to seek better "treasures" but rather to have one's allegiance to God and God's priorities as one's own priorities.

The eye in antiquity was viewed as the window on one's soul, so the reference here to the evil eye provides the clue for understanding verses 22-23, which are not just about stinginess. The point is that the whole life is clear or illuminated if one has singleness of purpose, has one's eye fixed on God's goal. Søren Kierkegaard put it this way: purity of heart is to will the one thing (necessary). By contrast when one has an eye that focuses on what is sick or bad, the soul becomes dark. The clue to the interpretation of the whole is found in verse 23c, "If the light which is in you is darkness, how great the darkness will be." Jesus is asking what is the central organizing principle and guiding light and orientation of your whole life. If one is fixed on God and the light of God, one's life will be enlightened.

Verse 24 brings this particular discussion to a climax. The point here is not that one could not work for two persons at the same time. The key here is the verb "to serve." One cannot give total and unconditional allegiance to two masters at once. One will be more devoted to one than the other, necessarily and unavoidably. And in any case, God will accept no competitors. He is either Lord of all in your life, or he is not Lord at all in your life. *Mammon* is an Aramaic term and does not actually mean "filthy lucre" or "ill-gotten gains"; it means possessions in general.[3] Earthly possessions can come to possess you, and you end up serving them rather than vice versa. Thus one becomes a slave to what one owns. It is not possible to be a slave of two masters at once and give them true service. But as Bob Dylan said in his famous song, we are indeed made to be servants of someone or something so we "have to serve somebody." We must choose *who* we will serve, not *whether* we will serve.

Matthew 6:25-34 corresponds to the petition about daily bread and involves a prohibition, support for the prohibition, and then an exhortation. Support for the initial prohibition comes from both nature and from human incapacity to change the length of one's life. The positive exhortation comes with a promise: God will supply what you need. Notice the initial prohibition of being anxiously concerned about basic things in life. Such anxiety leads not just to worry but to unnecessary activities to try to secure one's needs through one's own efforts. Jesus is not calling for his disciples to be careless, becoming reckless and irresponsible. He does not rule out forethought or planning, but he insists that faith, not fear and anxiety caused by fear, be the motivating force in deciding what we do and how we act. He also insists on leaving the results in God's hands. One is not to be anxious about one's life or life's basic necessities. If God can give you the greater gift of life itself, he can take care of the lesser gifts we need to sustain life. The illustration of the birds makes clear that God provides them with the place, means, and opportunities to feed themselves. The illustration from the wildflowers is similar. If God takes care of even the very contingent things like grass and flowers, how much more will he take care of those he created in his image? Bottom line: anxiety is a slap in the face of God, for it implicitly suggests, "I don't trust you, God, to take care of my life and its necessities."

Matthew 6:33 provides us with a familiar exhortation to seek first God's kingdom and his righteousness, and "all these things [the aforementioned necessities of life] will be given to you." This raises numerous questions. Does the word "first" suggest that if we put God first it is OK to be seeking these other things thereafter? It seems clear enough that the "these other things" are the one's previously mentioned—food, clothing, shelter. This is not a verse that justifies the health-and-wealth Gospel or the "God wants you rich" nonsense that is a perversion not a true version of the Gospel. In fact, the structure of the sentence suggests we should wholeheartedly seek the one thing, and God will take care of our needs. "Kingdom" here may refer to the future Kingdom yet to fully emerge on earth and final righteousness, or it may refer to what is already happening in our midst as God's saving reign breaks into our lives. In any case we are told to take it one day at a time—each day has enough troubles of its own.

Matthew 7 brings this longish discourse to a close focusing on some previously mentioned themes. Matthew 7:1-6 is certainly one of the more misunderstood portions of Jesus' teaching. In light of the other discourses in Matthew found on the lips of Jesus, it is quite impossible to argue that what Jesus means here is that one should never criticize anyone or anything. Nor is this a plea for Christians to avoid judging or critically evaluating persons and things, as 7:15-20, 10:11-15, 16:6-12, and 18:17-18 make very clear. The issue here has to do with unfair critiques, uncharitable evaluations, and especially judging others by a different standard than one uses to evaluate oneself. Crucial is the assertion that the disciple of Jesus will be judged by God using the same standard, criteria, critical scrutiny, and degree of probing he applies to others.

We need to keep steadily in view that the basic issue here is judging and condemning people themselves, not judging particular words or deeds of people. It is not for any human being to be the final arbiter or judge of another human being's life, nor do we have the right to assign anyone to outer darkness, making some kind of final spiritual judgment of them. The reason final judgment is to be left in God's hands is because only God (1) is all-seeing and all-knowing, knowing even the secrets of the heart, and (2) evaluates without bias—truly, fairly, and in accordance with the truth. One way to render the crucial saying here then would be, "Do not condemn another person to hell, so that you may avoid being similarly condemned at the last judgment." Notice as well in the illustration in verses 3-5 that the theme of hypocrisy crops up once again. Splinters or beams in the eyes stand for small or large moral oversights or defects. One is to first critically evaluate oneself and deal with one's own flaws before becoming a judge of others. Matthew 18:15-20 makes clear there is a place for correction of others, but not in a hypocritical fashion. The saying about casting pearls before swine in verse 6 reminds us that this is insider teaching for disciples, and it would be wasted on outsiders (pigs being a not infrequent and pejorative term for non-Jewish pagans).

In Matthew 7:7-14 we have brief sayings about seeking and asking for things from God, coupled with a reassurance that God is no prankster or gangster. He would not give a person a stone when he needed a loaf of bread. God doesn't play cruel games. The image of the disciple as the quester, the seeker who knocks on doors, is an image meant to suggest that disciples should live from a posture of trust. One should not start from a posture of pessimism or cynicism. The echo of the Lord's Prayer here is clearly reaffirming God as the one who provides. "All good things" here surely refers to both physical and spiritual goods. We need to bear in mind that whereas God always answers prayer he does sometimes answer no, which is indeed an answer to prayer. Disciples are called to trust themselves less and to trust God more. Verse 12 presents us with Jesus' version of the Golden Rule. Notice that Jesus assumes self-interest here and self-regard and seeks to stretch the audience toward self-sacrifice and love for others.

TWO FOUNDATIONS, ONE PARABLE

The final section of the Sermon on the Mount in 7:13-14 reminds us that the gate into the Kingdom has a narrow entrance, and the way into it is straight. One will either enter into the final dominion of God or into destruction, as Jesus puts it. Jesus is not a wide-eyed naive universalist. It is right to conclude that entering the Dominion here is seen as in the future, for entering into destruction is seen that way. One cannot enter into the Dominion without the greater righteousness, the bearing of good fruit, the doing of God's revealed will. Notice that Jesus even suggests that only few will enter that gate in due course. The implication is clearly that conduct after becoming a disciple can affect one's eternal destination. One is not eternally secure until one is securely in Eternity, in the Kingdom. It is easy to follow the broad way of the world now—harder to follow the Gospel way to the Kingdom. A tree that bears good fruit will be seen for what it is when the season for picking the fruit comes. But a tree that bears bad fruit will also be seen for what it is, and cut down (though the disciples are not called to be the lumberjacks). There is warning in 7:15-20 against false teachers and false prophets who lead even disciples astray.

Matthew 7:21-23 is interesting because the contrast here is not merely or mainly between walk and talk. The issue is whether a person has done God's will or not, even if they have performed miracles calling on the name of the Lord. Persons who have performed miracles are even said here to not make it into the Kingdom. Following and obeying Jesus and his teaching are the keys to entrance into the Kingdom. The sermon concludes with a parable in Matthew 7:24-29, a parable about the wise and foolish life. The parable is about hearing and putting into practice the teaching of Jesus. This is likened to building a house on solid rock. This suggests that the teaching in this sermon is viewed as foundational for the life of the disciple. One is not merely to know the foundational teachings of Jesus but to build a life on them. The disciples must live wisely with one eye on the horizon, for the Kingdom and final judgment is coming.

Notice that this final parable does not say or suggest that the person building on sand is building a different sort of house. He is just building on the wrong and unwise foundation. The two houses may appear identical, but they differ in a crucial respect: their foundations. My wife and I once lived in the caretaker's cottage next to Elvet Methodist Church in Durham, England. Unfortunately this cottage was half built on the unbiblical principle of sand, and so the left half was sinking into the parking lot! For three years my wife and I lived this parable while I was doing my PhD work. So much did the left side of the house lean that the upstairs bedroom had a slanted floor. Once, when my father got into bed in that room, he slid right through the bed and onto the floor with a thump. This parable reminds us, as do the sayings just before it, that belief without behavior is not true discipleship.

In the Sermon on the Mount, Jesus offers not so much a new law as new wisdom for living in the light of the coming Kingdom. This is wisdom grounded in his ministry and the new end-time situation he has brought about. New occasions teach new duties, and the truly wise person will follow not only the teaching of Jesus but also his personal example, for Jesus was not inclined to tell his disciples "go," but rather "come and follow me." He leads us all into the Kingdom, and he would not lead us anywhere that he had not gone first (see Hebrews 12:1-5).

To say the least, the teaching of Jesus in this so-called sermon is challenging. But at the same time we need to realize it does not provide a utopian ethic nor advice for only spiritual super athletes, but rather it addresses and assumes the real world with all its problems and promise, all its needs and wants. C. Bauman puts it this way:

The words of Jesus address a world where there is un-reconciled anger and litigations, adultery and divorce, where speech has lost its integrity, where there is persecution and retaliation, where coats are stolen and cheeks are slapped, where hatred of enemies is sanctioned, where hypocrisy parades in the guise of piety, where people trespass against each other and against God, where thieves break in and steal, and where there is danger of the whole body being full of darkness, where people are preoccupied with material cares and are anxious about the future, where they condemn each other and profane what is holy, and where the majority are on the way to destruction. Surely it is unrealistic to assume that the Sermon on the Mount applies only to an other-worldly apocalyptic or monastic ideal where these conditions presumably don't apply.[4]

This is an ethic for those on the journey through the world into God's kingdom, an ethic for behavior after one has safely arrived in that final Kingdom. As such, it is a wisdom that the world would not call wisdom, but disciples should recognize it as such, for it reflects the life Jesus himself, the Wisdom of God, lived every single day of his life.

NOTES

1. Robert A. Guelich, *The Sermon on the Mount: A Foundation for Understanding* (Nashville: W. Publishing Group, 1982), 38.

2. David Hill, *The Gospel of Matthew*, The New Century Bible Commentary (Grand Rapids: Eerdmans, 1972), 56.

3. See Ben Witherington III, *Jesus and Money: A Guide for Times of Financial Crisis* (Grand Rapids: Brazos, 2010).

4. Clarence Bauman, *The Sermon on the Mount: The Modern Quest for Its Meaning* (Macon: Mercer University Press, 1985), 409.

CHAPTER THREE

JESUS' SOCIAL NETWORK

*Christ's preaching threatens men, the virtuous even more
than the wicked, with a radical transformation of values
whereby the rich and the pious are damned, and the har-
lots and tax collectors are rather more acceptable. . . .
Two worlds are colliding; amazement prevails. . . . This
kingdom is the hope and pain of Christianity; it is
attained against the grain, through the denial of instinct
and social wisdom and through faith in the unseen.*

—John Updike[1]

It is an odd fact, but nonetheless a fact, that not many scholars
have evaluated Jesus on the basis of his relationships—his relationships with John the Baptizer, his disciples, his family, the
Pharisees and Sadducees, foreigners. In short, there have not
been many good treatments of Jesus and his social network—who
did he befriend, and who became foes? Who understood the
most, and who understood him least? What sort of people did he
socialize with, and what sort of places and persons did he avoid?
In our first study, we examined Jesus in his relationships with his
family and with his disciples, but here we must expand that to see
how Jesus related to others outside his family and the family of
faith. I find it odd that this has not been more closely evaluated

not least because ancient cultures did not work like modern Western individualistic societies.

What I mean by that last sentence is that although Jesus' world was populated by individuals, it was not populated by individualists. Indeed, "just being yourself" was not really seen as normal at all. The dominant identity type was group identity. We should have realized this when we noticed that people in Jesus' world did not have last names. I trust you know that "Christ" was not Jesus' last name, nor for that matter was "Magdalene" Mary's last name. Personality and identity were assumed to be largely determined by geography, gender, generation. That is to say, where you came from, what sex you were (in a dominantly patriarchal culture), and who your father was were all thought to determine one's identity from birth. Life was not about finding yourself but recognizing the social network and family and tribe in which you were embedded from day one. You were born with this identity, and you were stuck with it for life.

Scholars call this sort of corporate or group identity "dyadic personality." This means that a person's identity is formed by the group one is a part of, and by no means does one want to stand out from the crowd. That would be odd and abnormal. In a limited sense, ancient identity was like modern teenagers trying to fit into a clique or particular group at school or like gang identity. You didn't want to look different, dress different, act different; you just wanted to belong, to fit in.

When someone like Jesus came along, someone who didn't seem to fit in very well with his family or his hometown extended family and friends, or even with other very religious people of his day such as the Pharisees, people tended to view that person as strange and hold him or her at arm's length. And, indeed, this often happened to Jesus. He was often on the road, even trying to get away from the miracle-hungry crowds, and at one point he laments that the Son of Man has nowhere to lay his head. If not an outcast, Jesus was definitely an outsider or a misfit to all sorts of groups in his world. This is all the more reason why analyzing Jesus in his relationships is so critical to understanding both the man and his mission and ministry.

JESUS AND JOHN

In one sense, the most important and revealing relationship in Jesus' young adult life and at the start of his ministry is the relationship with his cousin, John the Baptizer, who had a vital and notable prophetic ministry before Jesus had any ministry at all. Indeed, in all four Gospels when the Gospel writers begin to talk about the beginnings of Jesus' ministry they feel compelled to talk about John the Baptizer first. He, in one sense, is seen as the beginning of the story of the Good News, the one who sets things in motion and prepares Israel for the inbreaking of God's dominion. This positive view of John is not just because in reality he was very important but also because Jesus saw John as a positive and important figure in early Judaism. Indeed at one point he called him "the greatest person ever born of woman"!

On the one hand, John appears rather like an Old Testament prophet, in particular Elijah, in his dress and diet and political message. Like Elijah, he gets in trouble with the local Jewish ruler, with Herod Antipas and Herodias playing the latter-day parts of Ahab and Jezebel who tried to do away with Elijah. And, in fact, Jesus himself sees John as an Elijah-like figure. But John is not, unlike the Pharisees, just a reformer of society, because he calls even the ritually pure to be baptized and to repentance. He denies that descent from Abraham is any protection against the coming judgment. And unlike Jesus, John performs no controversial miracles; indeed, he performs no miracles at all that we know of. Jesus on the other hand, according to John 4, baptized no one. In short, Jesus and John are closely linked but distinguishable. One could say they were linked from birth, as both were the product of miraculous pregnancies.

Many scholars have noted the similarities between John and the Qumran community and its leader, the Teacher of Righteousness. John is out by the Jordan and in the chalk wilderness near the Jordan. He engages in water rituals like the Qumran community, and like some of them he is ascetical in his piety. Furthermore, the Scripture used in the Gospels to characterize

John and his ministry from Isaiah 40—"the voice of one crying, in the wilderness make straight a highway for our God"—was in fact a sort of theme verse for the Qumran community by the Dead Sea. That was precisely what they were doing out there: preparing the way for the coming of God and his judgment on a corrupt Temple and priestly hierarchy. But John, when we meet him, is not part of that community.

John emerges as a young and fearless prophet, standing alone at the Jordan, baptizing for repentance and not mincing words about leaders who are more like vipers than victors or heroes. What needs to be stressed about John's ministry is that he is offering an alternative way of forgiveness. You don't have to go to the Temple and offer a sacrifice. You can come to John, be baptized, and get forgiveness. No wonder even tax collectors and soldiers were coming to John and getting in the water with him (compare Matthew 21:31-32; Luke7:29-30).

One of the major differences between John and Jesus, besides the fact that the former baptized people and the latter did not, is that John seems to have definitely expected a successor whereas Jesus did not. John expected someone to come after him, whether a messianic figure or God himself, to bring in the judgment and pruning and purifying of God's people. The problem with Jesus was that he came proclaiming good news and healing people. This was not quite what John expected, as we shall see. In any case, John did not see himself as the definitive and final act in the salvation history drama of God's people. Someone or something would come after him. This also means that John did not see himself in a messianic light. He was the one who prepared the way, and he was not worthy even to tie the sandal of the one who would follow him. The successor would baptize with Spirit and fire; John simply baptized with water.

The sermon of John recorded in Matthew 3 and Luke3:1-22 is a substantial one and presents John as warning of the wrath to come, calling various Jewish leaders snake spawn (not exactly the way to curry favor with religious leaders). He also warned that what would come after would be a more substantial baptism of Spirit and fire, and the one who did that would "clear his threshing floor and will gather his wheat into the granary, but the chaff he will burn with unquenchable fire" (Matthew 3:12). John's colorful prediction has all sorts of end-time overtones, and doubtless he believes what the Old Testament said about the judgment of God beginning with the household of God. To whom more is given, more is expected. One may compare John's sermon with Jesus' parable of the wheat and tares or the parable of the net (Matthew 13:24b, 26b, 30b). This makes clear that both John and Jesus (1) proclaimed the imminent intervention of God's final judgment and reign on the earth and (2) called for an immediate response to coming judgment so that one might avoid being placed in the chaff pile and being burned up in the coming conflagration. Further, John believes that Israel, or at least its leadership, is deeply corrupted, and Jesus is said to have called all Israel or a significant portion of it "the lost sheep of Israel."

If initially John viewed Jesus, at his baptism, as the Coming One, even perhaps as God's Lamb who takes away sins, it is clear enough from Matthew 11:2-19 and Luke 7:18-35 that, later on, John had some doubts about who Jesus really was. His ministry didn't seem to involve judgment but rather healings and good news. So we have the tale of John, incarcerated by Herod Antipas the ruler of Galilee, sending some of his disciples to Jesus to ask the question: "Are you the one who is to come, or should we look for another?" Jesus by contrast seems to have no doubts about John and the authenticity of his prophetic ministry and message—he thinks it is of God and points rightly to the coming reign of God.

Jesus' response to John's question from prison involves a composite citation of bits from Isaiah 26:19; 29:18-19; 35:5-6; and 61:1. The citation makes clear that Jesus sees himself as not merely a giver of prophecy, like John, but rather a fulfiller of it. And the fulfillment of these sorts of prophecies should be seen as signs of the coming messianic age, brought in by Jesus himself. What is interesting about this citation, and also the one from Isaiah 61 in Luke 4, is that Jesus leaves out the references to vengeance in Isaiah 29:20; 35:5; and 61:2. Rather, he stresses healing and the blessings that come upon those who neither find no offense in nor stumble because of what Jesus is doing and who he is. Jesus' answer to John is of course indirect, but it is not obscure. Jesus allows his deeds and words about the good news of the inbreaking of the Dominion to reveal who he is, to John as well as to others. We are not told how John responded to Jesus' answer. Indeed, the next thing we know, John is off the scene, and Jesus stands alone as a prophetic or end-time figure. But we can learn more about Jesus himself from the way he characterized John.

In Matthew 11:7-11 and Luke 7:24-28, John is characterized as the greatest person ever born of woman (although Jesus adds that the least in the Kingdom is greater than him), and John is said to be more than an ordinary prophet. In fact, Jesus seems to suggest that John fits the role of the Elijah figure mentioned in Malachi 3:1 (compare Exodus 23:20), the one who comes before the "great and terrible Day of Yahweh." But if Jesus saw John as the final great end-time prophet, how then did he view himself? Apparently he viewed himself as transcending prophetic categories, and moving into messianic ones—he is the one who fulfills the prophecies. John is viewed by Jesus as a transitional figure with one foot in each age: this age and the age to come. The time of the Law and the Prophets was ceasing to be. The time of the fulfillment of all things was beginning.

Matthew 11:16-19 and Luke 7:31-35 conclude this section, and here we learn that the style of Jesus' ministry was contrasted by him with the style of John's ministry. It seems that "this generation" is not pleased with the ascetical ministry of John or the more convivial one of Jesus. The audience of Jesus and John would neither mourn nor party and dance with them. They were not pleased with solemnity or with joy. John is seen as a fanatic with a demon. Jesus is seen as immoral and a libertine (not only a glutton and a drunkard but a friend of such people, of people who should be shunned—sinners, tax collectors, and the like). It is clear from a saying like this that Jesus and John had different visions of how to go about their ministries, and so their practice varied. Jesus sees John as revealing God's wisdom, pointing to it, but he sees himself as the embodiment or incarnation of God's wisdom, whose character can be known by the deeds done.

Finally, if we consider a text like John 3:22–4:9, we learn a few interesting things about Jesus. First, of course, Jesus endorsed John's ministry, and some of his own disciples had first been John's disciples, which may be why some of Jesus' disciples practiced baptism (whereas Jesus did not). Second, Jesus stayed with John in Perea beyond the Jordan for a considerable period of time, which led to the speculation that he might have been a follower of John for a time. Jesus' inaugural message according to Mark 1:15 was the same as John's: repent for the divine saving activity, the reign of God is inbreaking. But Jesus apparently did not engage full-scale in his ministry until John was off the scene.

John the Baptizer is for Jesus the touchstone, if not the loadstone, of his ministry. If you want to understand Jesus, you must understand the positive relationship he had with John, and yet you must also understand how his own ministry was distinguishable from John's, though sometimes confused. (Remember Mark 8 where the disciples say that some think Jesus is John back from the dead.) Jesus believed John's water baptism was a valid and valuable practice, but something greater was coming after that practice involving God's Spirit, and Jesus was the one bringing in that saving action.

JESUS AND THE PHARISEES

Pharisaism was the most popular and prominent of early Jewish religious groups both before and after the destruction of the Temple in A.D. 70. Indeed, all post-70 Jewish groups and movements are the offspring of that movement, including most all forms of modern Judaism.[2] It has been said that Pharisaism, while having only a small number of card-carrying members, so to speak, was nonetheless the voice of the people in Jesus' day, the group most admired and looked to for religious leadership in Jesus' day. Pharisaism was a holiness movement, and in a sense, the Jesus movement was its closest competitor in that regard. Like Jesus, Pharisees believed some significant things were wrong in Israel, and their solution was a closer adherence not just to the Mosaic law but to the traditions of the elders—a whole series of amplifying comments and interpretations of that law. There seems to have been a particular concern with boundary-defining ritual law—having to do with circumcision, Sabbath observance, food laws, hand washing, Corban,[3] tithing, and the like. In other words, they were very concerned about the things that most distinguished and set apart Jews from other people, including other very religious people. The Pharisaic solution to the problems in Israel was a more intense degree of devotion and adherence to Levitical law and more broadly the law found in the Mosaic covenant, as interpreted through the legal traditions of the Pharisees.

Because of the intense concern with orthopraxy, the doing of the law exactly and precisely correctly, Pharisees are often found in tandem with scribes in the Gospels. The Pharisees are just pious laypersons, but the scribes are the theologians and scholars, the one's tasked with the precise interpretation of Scripture. (Compare Mark 3:22; Matthew 8:19; 9:14; 13:52. Mark 2:16 even refers to the scribes of the Pharisees.) The term *Pharisee* seems to come from *perushim*, referring to those who have set themselves apart from less observant Jews.

The goal of the Pharisees was "to spread Scriptural holiness throughout the land," to borrow a phrase from eighteenth-century English revivals. According to the Pharisees, oral Torah (law) was passed on through Moses to God's people along with the written Torah, and one needed to observe both to be a good, ritually pure Jew. And the Pharisees believed their scribes knew the oral Torah better than anyone. This in turn led to the surprising outcome that oral Torah became more normative in some respects than even the written Torah. The Mishnah[4] later explained, "It is more culpable to teach against the ordinances of the scribes than against the Torah itself." Politics was not the main concern or focus of the Pharisees. They were neither Sadducees nor Zealots, on the whole. They were only concerned

with politics if politics somehow got in the way of Torah observance as they thought it should be observed. So popular were the
Pharisees that even the Sadducean priests in the Temple offered
their sacrifices according to the Pharisaic interpretations of how
the animals should be slaughtered and the sacrifices offered. The
Pharisees sought the hallowing of every aspect of every day
through meticulous observance of the law but within the existing
structure of society, not apart from it, as the Qumran community
did.

It probably goes without saying that: (1) Jesus, while he agreed
with the Pharisees in some of his theological and ethical views
(for example, resurrection and angels and demons), was not a
Pharisee. (2) We regularly see Jesus having heated debates with
Pharisees, though his relationship with some of them is not
adversarial. (3) At times Jesus could even commend the
Pharisees' teaching and righteousness (for example, Matthew
23:3), but more often than not he seemed to be at odds with
them for a variety of reasons. The Pharisees strongly objected to:
(1) Jesus having table fellowship with tax collectors and those
they deemed notorious sinners and unclean people; (2) some of
the things Jesus did on the Sabbath, including some healings; (3)
the practice of Jesus' disciples when it came to gleaning from a
field on the Sabbath and hand washing. Not incidentally, the
Pharisees almost always appear in controversy dialogues in the
Gospels.

Mark 7 becomes a crucial text for understanding what created
the animus between Jesus and the Pharisees. If Jesus did indeed
say that what goes in a person's mouth does not defile them, then
there would be a strong disagreement with the Pharisees on the
issue of unclean food (see Mark 7:15-19). This was no small matter, because it also helped to determine whether one could eat
with Gentiles in Gentile houses where kosher was not kept. In
Mark 7:7-8 Jesus objects to the upholding of the oral Torah at the
expense of the written Torah itself. Jesus calls the oral Torah
merely human interpretations. One could also conclude from
some of the antitheses in Matthew 5:21 and the following verses
that Jesus rejected oral Torah and the traditions of the elders in

various regards. I have argued elsewhere that Mark 7:15 does indeed go back to Jesus himself, in which case he is saying that Leviticus 11 and Deuteronomy 14 no longer apply to his disciples in the current end-time situation. Jesus is not concerned with what goes into the mouth so much as what comes out of it: words that curse and defile. Likewise, Jesus is more concerned with what goes into and comes out of the human heart than what physically goes into and comes out of the human body. There is some truth to the notion that he is concerned with moral purity—extremely so—rather than ritual purity. The Pharisees were concerned with both. But what most seemed to gall the Pharisees about Jesus is that he seemed to assume he had the authority to change the rules, to reinterpret the tradition, and even to say which parts of the Torah were and weren't still binding, at least for his own disciples. In other words, he treated Torah with sovereign freedom.

If we turn to one of the major bones of contention—Jesus' approach to the Sabbath—things become clearer. Mark 2:23-28 illustrates the sort of controversy the behavior of Jesus and his disciples caused. It will be noted from the outset that the basic assumption, which Jesus himself accepts, is that he is responsible for the behavior of his disciples. Indeed, he provides a justification for the behavior of his disciples rather than correction. The bone of contention is not *that* the gleaning happened but rather *when* it happened. The appeal to the example of David and the showbread suggests that Jesus sees the times are such that this kind of behavior is justified and should not be condemned.

To be clear, the Pharisees are right that Exodus 16:25-26 would seem to rule out this sort of behavior on the Sabbath. The issue here then is not mere oral tradition but what the Torah itself says, as was the case with the material in Mark 7. Jesus is making the major point that people do not exist for the sake of the law, but rather the law exists for the sake of the people. And, furthermore, the Sabbath exists for the restoration and rest of the people. In Jesus' view, the Sabbath is the perfect day to heal someone and give them rest from what ails them. Similarly, the hungry disciples should be able to eat like they did on the

Sabbath, as it was meant for their rest and good health. In other words, Jesus seeks to interpret Torah in light of (1) what he sees as its true intent and (2) the new end-time situation.

It is appropriate to ask at this juncture, what sort of person thinks he can say that this portion of Scripture no longer applies or that this portion of Scripture must be interpreted differently? One is confronted with the conclusion that either Jesus saw himself as standing above the law and using it to fit his mission and end-time vision of the situation, or he was a lawbreaker. The Pharisees thought the latter, whereas the disciples of Jesus came to the former conclusion. It needs to be stressed, however, that the issue here is not legalism versus a free-wheeling interpretation of the law. Jesus was just as much a moral rigorist as the Pharisees were about some things, such as marriage and divorce, and the issue is not just ritual versus moral law. It is more complex than that. Jesus has no problems with participating in weddings or festivals or prayers and the like.

It seems that the Pharisees objected to both the lack of fasting by Jesus' disciples and the feasting that Jesus seems to have done with tax collectors and notable sinners. It is clear enough that fasting was a practice stressed by the Pharisees (Luke 18:12). It is notable that Jesus in Mark 2:18-22 suggests that fasting is not really all that appropriate at wedding time—when the bridegroom is present. This involves an implicit messianic claim that Jesus seems to have been making. The Kingdom is coming, and it's time to celebrate not to fast. Jesus sees himself as bringing about a new and different and joyous set of affairs. In regard to feasting with the ne'er-do-wells in Mark 2:15-17 (compare Matthew 11:19; Luke 7:34), the term "sinner" probably refers to the morally suspect or even the openly immoral, not to everyone as it did in later Christian literature. Jesus says he came to call and redeem such people, and one way he did this was by building a relationship with them through dining with them.

Tax collectors were Jews who were considered traitors, or betrayers of their own people—especially if they worked directly for the Romans. It is striking that sinners and tax collectors are grouped together in a number of texts (Luke 15:2; Matthew

11:19; Mark 2:16 and the parallels in Matthew and Luke). Jesus apparently fraternized with such people enough to cause a scandal. Thus his behavior toward sinners, his behavior on the Sabbath, his pronouncement by what counted as unclean and clean all would have set off alarm bells for Pharisees and been seen as a direct contradiction of what they were trying to accomplish with the people, and perhaps even as a threat to the survival of the people, because in their view it represented blatant unfaithfulness to God and disobedience to his eternal law. The irony is that in his largely adversarial relationship with Pharisees (there were exceptions, such as Nicodemus), Jesus saw the Pharisaic approach to holiness and the law as the real threat to both the unity and internal cohesion of God's people and to their survival in the face of the judgment that would fall on them through the Jewish war leading to the destruction of the Temple itself.

The saying in Mark 2:17a speaks volumes about Jesus' self-understanding and why he did what he did. He came to seek and to save the least, the last, the lost. He knew that as a physician he would have to do some things that crossed some lines, particular purity lines, such as a physician who has to risk catching the patient's disease to cure them. Presumably banqueting with the bad and laying hands on the sick and calling sinners with the intent of turning them into disciples were bridges too far for the Pharisees. This is not because they were hypocrites, as a group, but because they were so profoundly and deeply committed to Torah and assumed their own interpretation of it was necessarily the right one. In other words, they were like fundamentalists in their exclusive ways of interpreting the Scriptures.

JESUS AND THE SADDUCEES

It has been regularly noticed that Jesus does not seem to have a lot of interaction with Sadducees before we get to the last week of his life. In most respects, this is unsurprising. The Sadducees were the nobility who lived in and around Jerusalem, and who were related to and connected with the priestly hierarchy. The Sadducees could be said to have embraced "that ol' time religion" following exactly what the Mosaic law said, rather strictly interpreted. They did not agree with the Pharisees about the oral tradition and its supposed moral authority, and they disagreed on doctrinal matters as well, not accepting things such as the idea of bodily resurrection. It may seem strange to us, but in many ways the Pharisees were perceived as the broader minded Jewish religious leaders, as the oral tradition often found ways of ameliorating the harshness of the literal interpretation of the Mosaic law. The Sadducees did not usually agree with this sort of watering down of Moses' dictums. In order to understand something of the relationship of the Sadducees and Pharisees, a brief bit of history is in order.

The Pharisees and the Sadducees begin to show up as distinguishable religious sects in the beginning of the second century B.C. The term *Sadducee* seems to come from the priestly name and line of Zadok. Josephus the Jewish historian tells us that they were the socially elite echelon of Judaean society, and they were deeply involved in politics and the building and maintaining of the Temple precincts. One way to summarize what they did is as follows. They:

- administered the state domestically,
- represented the state internationally,
- collected taxes (which also came in the form of international tribute from Jews in the Diaspora),
- administered justice,
- equipped and led armies,
- regulated relations with the Romans,
- resolved misunderstandings, and
- mediated grievances.[5]

Besides not believing in the oral tradition or the resurrection, Josephus also says that the Sadducees did not believe in fate (that is, predestination), nor did they believe God was the author of evil, rather they believed in human free will, and they believed that this life was the sum total of existence—there was no immortal soul nor any reward or punishment in the afterlife (see Josephus's *Antiquities* 18:1-4). This quite readily brings us to the famous story of Jesus' confrontation with the Sadducees about Levirate marriage, but we need to bear in mind that it was especially Sadducees in the Sanhedrin, and most prominently the high priests Annas and Caiaphas, who would have most objected to Jesus' actions in the Temple, for they saw themselves as its guardians.

Matthew 22:23-33 tells us that Sadducees confronted Jesus during the last week of his life in Jerusalem and asked him a question about Levirate marriage, an issue they thought still important, even though it appears that the practice of Levirate marriage was largely in abeyance by Jesus' day (see Deuteronomy 25:5-10). They may be drawing on a preexisting Jewish tale (from the Apocryphal book of Tobit 3:7-10). But the real reason they raise the issue with Jesus is that they see a chance to dispute the notion of resurrection with Jesus, since he believes in it. The question raised is surely hypothetical, in view of the disuse of the practice in Jesus' day and also the number of brothers involved in the example. Is it really to be believed that one woman married seven brothers from one family just so a male heir could be produced?

The case involves seven brothers who had tried and failed to impregnate the woman in question. But she had outlived them all and was single when she died. It is this last fact, her current singleness, which likely prompts the question: Whose spouse will she be in the resurrection? The Sadducees' answer was of course no one's since she won't be raised and won't be alive then. But there is also the assumption that if there is such an afterlife in the resurrection, it will have complete continuity with this life in terms of its conditions. Apparently, the idea here is: How can anyone believe in a ridiculous notion like resurrection if it produces one wife having seven husbands?

Jesus' response begins at Matthew 22:29 and suggests that the Sadducees are ignorant of both the content of the Scriptures and the power of God. Jesus stresses that the conditions that produced Levirate marriage will no longer exist in the age to come. Levirate marriage exists because death exists. But in the resurrection there is no more death and dying, hence no more need for Levirate marriage. It is important to realize that Jesus does not say, "There will be no more marriage in the life to come"—though that may be true as well—but "there will be no more marrying (a male act) and giving in marriage (what happened to the betrothed woman) in the age to come." There will be no new marriages in the end-time state. This did not mean all marriages would disappear, although elsewhere in the New Testament that seems to be the implication (see Romans 7:1-4 and 1 Corinthians 7). In any case, in the resurrection people no longer die, and Levirate marriage was founded on the reality of death. Had Jesus answered the question directly he could have said, "Only the first marriage still stands, as only the first marriage was not undertaken to produce an heir after the husband died." Jesus adds that in the end-time state, we will be like angels, which does not mean we will be gender neutral but rather that we will be deathless, like the angels, who were indeed viewed as sexual beings by early Jews (see Genesis 6:1-4 and 1 Peter 3). Jesus then seems to have distinguished between ordinary marriage and Levirate marriage, as most early Jews did.

The argument used to support the resurrection in verses 31-32 is also interesting. Jesus argues that the references to God being the God of Abraham, Isaac, and Jacob suggests that those three patriarchs survived death, contrary to what Sadducees thought (compare 4 Maccabees 7:19; 16:25; and Luke 16 on Abraham in paradise). Jesus is perhaps arguing that since many of the promises to the patriarchs had not yet been fulfilled, that there must be a resurrected state in which they will be fulfilled to them.

Jesus accuses the Sadducees not only of bad interpretation of Scripture but of a failure of nerve, a failure to believe either in the power of God or in the ability of God to extend life into an afterlife on this earth by means of resurrection. The sort of resurrection the Sadducees believed in—raising up an heir for a deceased brother—was but a pale shadow of the sort Jesus believed in—a miraculous raising from the dead of the deceased himself. When we combine this argument with Jesus' action in the Temple, it is easy to see why the Sadducees might not be inclined to acquit Jesus of charges or accusations before the Sanhedrin at the end of the week of Passover. But that action of Jesus in the Temple raised other kinds of questions about him as well: was he a Zealot?

JESUS AND THE ZEALOTS

The phrase "Jesus was a revolutionary" has been thrown around a lot, with a variety of possible meanings. Sometimes the phrase is modified to "Jesus was a nonviolent revolutionary," but then the question becomes, What does the term *revolutionary* actually mean in such a phrase? If Jesus is not like Che Gueverra, what sort of revolutionary was he, or was he a revolutionary at all? One way to frame this question is to ask about Jesus' relationship with actual revolutionaries of his day. Was Jesus a Zealot? Let's be clear that there were definitely revolutionaries around in the era in which Jesus lived. Judas the Galilean in about A.D. 6 led a revolt against the census of Quirinius and the Roman taxes that were to follow. He broke into the armory in Sepphoris near Nazareth. He was like other Zealots, in favor of the violent overthrow of the Romans and perhaps also their puppet or client kings, such as Herod Antipas. Some of the Zealots were in fact theocrats in the true sense—they believed in a theocracy, only God should rule the Jewish people as in the time of Joshua. Josephus tells us that Judas and his descendants planted the seeds for the later revolutionary actions during the Jewish wars in the 60s (*Antiquities* 17–18).

Jesus may not have ministered in a regularly violent environment, but the situation was definitely volatile, and the taxation issues were a tipping point over and over again. It is no surprise at all that Jesus is asked about paying taxes to Caesar. It is a surprise perhaps that Jesus seems to have picked two Zealots to be in his inner circle: Simon the Zealot and Judas Iscariot. We will speak more about that later in this chapter. Besides the Freedom Fighters, there were also various messianic figures in the era of Jesus. Besides Jesus, during the reign of Pilate, there was the figure called the Samaritan, who had drawn great crowds and promised to reveal the sacred Mosaic vessels on Mount Gerizim. Pilate's response to such things was typically even less restrained than Herod Antipas—he would simply repress such movements violently. It could be a dangerous thing in Jesus' day to suggest one was the messiah, much less suggest one was a Zealot as well. And make no mistake, when Jesus turned over the tables of the money changers in the temples and let a few animals loose and apparently said something like "Zeal for thy house consumed me," there were plenty of Passover pilgrims in Jerusalem then ready to read those actions in a revolutionary way. But of course there were many different images of and ideas about messiah in early Judaism, and only one of them involved seeing the messiah as some sort of military figure like David who would come and clean out the land of foreigners by force (see the Jewish work the Psalms of Solomon 17–18). Jesus, if he saw himself in a messianic way, and he did, would have to take care in how he presented himself if he did not want to be seen as a violent revolutionary or a militaristic messiah.

We have already looked at Jesus' call to nonresistance in the Sermon on the Mount, which does not encourage us to see Jesus as a Zealot if by that one means a revolutionary prepared to use violence to attain his aims. There are a series of texts, however, that we need to consult to sort out Jesus' views more clearly.

The first of these, found in Mark 12:13-17 is the famous "render unto Caesar" text. Everything in the story prepares the way for the famous saying of Jesus that concludes the story and is unanswerable. It is obviously quite believable that anyone as controversial as Jesus would be likely to be asked the question about paying taxes. It was a burning issue, especially when it came to tribute money paid to Caesar, but even the Temple tax caused some grumbling as well.

The coin in question, with the head of Tiberius on it, was inscribed "High Priest" (back) and "Tiberius Caesar, son of the divine Augustus" (front). Even to have such a coin would be seen as a form of idolatry to many devout Jews. And notice that Jesus does not have such a coin on his person. It is entirely likely that this question was raised while Jesus was in Judaea since Judaea was ruled directly by a Roman procurator—Pontius Pilate. Judas the Galilean, a revolutionary during Jesus' youth, said it was immoral or sacrilegious to pay tribute money to Caesar. So the probing question was to try to force Jesus to lay his cards on the table. Did he agree with the revolutionaries on this matter or not?

The phrase "is it permitted to pay" indicates that the question has to do with whether Mosaic law permits such paying of tribute money. Jesus' direct response presupposes that the audience knows that, in fact, the person who mints the coins, owns the coins, is Caesar. Jesus, it will be remembered, seemed not to have a very high regard for money anyway, calling it "unrighteous mammon" (Luke 16:9; Mark 10:25).[6] In fact, Jesus saw money as a possible impediment to entering the kingdom of God (Mark 10:25; Luke 16:19-31). It is thus very unlikely that Jesus means by his famous saying, "Be civic minded and pay your taxes." Nor is it at all likely that Jesus is endorsing a two-spheres idea (one kingdom of Caesar over here, one kingdom of God over there). He is not talking about the separation of church and state either. There was no church as of yet when he uttered this famous saying. What then is Jesus saying?

Let it be said first that since Jesus believed that the kingdom of God was already breaking into the present, it is unlikely that Jesus here is giving some sort of wholehearted endorsement of Rome and its taxes. But it seems equally clear that since he says pay the tribute money, revolutionaries would have seen this as an unacceptable compromise. But Jesus believed that paying taxes neither helped nor hindered the coming of the kingdom of God. Nothing could prevent that occurring. Paying taxes then could not be some sort of ultimate litmus test of one's loyalty to God and God's word.

Here then seems to be what Jesus means: if one renders to God what is God's and in the end everything belongs to the Creator

God, then Caesar really has no claim on anything. But since Jesus says give Caesar back his coins, it could mean refuse to have anything to do with such money with their graven images. But this ironic saying, which would mean "give Caesar back his worthless pieces of metal" would give the Herodians, Pharisees, and Sadducees no reason to report Jesus to Rome on this score.

Perhaps, however, we should focus on the question that Jesus raises, "Whose image is on the coin?" Is this a saying about contrasting the image of God in oneself with the image of Caesar on the coin? If that is the case, then finally we can make sense of this whole saying: "Give Caesar back his worthless pieces of metal with his image on it, but give your whole self to God because you bear God's image." Here is a saying that entirely satisfies neither Caesar nor the Zealots. But what it does do is make clear that Jesus was miles apart from the revolutionaries in this matter.

Our next text of importance in this discussion is the story of Jesus' grand entrance into Jerusalem on what Christians now call Palm Sunday (Mark 11:1-11 and the parallels in Matthew and Luke). What did it mean for Jesus to get on the back of a donkey to the cries of "Hosanna" and "Blessed is he who comes in the name of the Lord" and ride into town? There is little doubt that the story is told with one eye on the prophetic text in Zechariah 9, though the Hallel songs[7] that pilgrims sang coming into Jerusalem included precisely these sorts of acclamations, whether or not Jesus was coming into town. More interesting is the waving of palm branches, which was a symbol of the Maccabean victory when they finally retook Jerusalem a couple of centuries earlier. The real question is, What did Jesus intend by riding into town this way, and did he personally have Zechariah 9 in mind?

The first thing to notice is that Jesus does not enter the city on a war horse (contrast Psalms of Solomon 17–18) or like King David as a conquering hero. Jesus rides into town on a donkey, and what Zechariah says about such a king is that he is a king of peace, a shepherd king. This comports with what Jesus says at the Last Supper, again with a quote from Zechariah, "I will strike the shepherd and the sheep will scatter" (Mark 14:27; Zechariah 13:7). Jesus again refuses to present himself as a militaristic figure, relying instead on more pacific images of a king, but this gesture of riding into town on a donkey (which was how about-to-be-crowned Solomon rode into Jerusalem), deliberately elevating himself above the crowd for the first time in his ministry, must be seen as significant, not least because of the timing of the event. It was the week of Passover, when Jerusalem's population swelled from fifty thousand to near five hundred thousand. It was the highest visibility occasion Jesus could have picked to do such a thing. Jesus then reveals his messianic self-understanding here, but in perhaps the least expected form. He has not come to chase the Romans out of town. But has he come to clean house—the house of God—and chase the Jewish authorities out of town? We must consider another text at this juncture.

Without question, the action of Jesus that has most prompted the suggestion that Jesus was a revolutionary who would resort to some forms of violence is the story of his action in the Temple, told in all four Gospels. And indeed, this action is characterized in part by an Old Testament saying near and dear to the Zealots: "Zeal for my house has consumed me, says the LORD." There can be no doubt as well that the Dead Sea community thought that Herod's Temple was hopelessly corrupt and would be judged; but did Jesus agree, and did he see himself as the judge who came to town to do the judging?

One of the possible keys to understanding the story in Mark 11 (and the parallels in Matthew and Luke) is that the advent of changing money and selling animals in the outer court of the Temple, the court of the Gentiles, was recent. Jesus may have been suggesting by his action that this new economic move by the High Priest and his hierarchy, so they could make more money, was the object of Jesus' ire, not the Temple itself. On this view, Jesus came to cleanse the corruption from the Temple, not to suggest it should be dismantled much less that he would dismantle it. There is however a problem with this view. It doesn't fit all the evidence. For example, if Jesus intended to actually cleanse the Temple, his action was too limited to accomplish such an aim—it involved a few animals and a few money changers' coins. Business as usual could have resumed moments later or never have stopped in the rest of the court. Jesus' action has to be seen as a prophetic sign act, and so as symbolic, not as an actual cleansing of the Temple per se. But what did it symbolize?

The second thing to point out is that elsewhere (Mark 13 and the parallels in Matthew and Luke) Jesus certainly did tell his disciples that this Temple was the Temple of Doom. It was going to be destroyed within a generation. And sure enough it was destroyed in exactly a biblical generation, forty years later in A.D. 70. And at Jesus' trial, he is accused of threatening to destroy the Temple himself, though that seems to be based on a misinterpretation of his enigmatic phrase, "Destroy this temple, and it will be raised in three days." Additionally, we need to take into account the accusation that the Temple is supposed to be a house of prayer but that, instead, it has been turned into a den of robbers.

On the whole it seems we are left with two choices, neither of which amount to Jesus taking violent action to destroy the Temple itself. (1) Jesus took no action against human beings but rather against two buying or exchanging activities, so his action could be seen as a prophetic sign act of the coming judgment on the Temple. Or (2) Jesus, perhaps slightly more likely, was condemning corruption, new economic practices, in the Temple, and so it was a sign act against such corruption, a sign of the need for cleansing, not a prophetic sign of destruction of the Temple itself. Either way, Jesus is not leading the Zealots into the Temple and trying to tear it down. His action is a prophetic sign act foreshadowing God's action. Jesus' zeal consumed him, and he would go on to die on a cross; it did not consume the Temple, as the later fire in A.D. 70 did. But Jesus was right: the doom of this Temple was sure, not least because the corruption continued after his death, and during the Jewish war it really did become a den or haven of bandits, robbers, thieves, and Zealots.

AND SO?

What we have seen in this chapter by examining Jesus in the context of his relationships with groups beyond his most intimate circles is that controversy swirled around Jesus regardless of who confronted him—Pharisees, Sadducees, Zealots, or Temple authorities. It is not a surprise that in the end he was still aggravating authority figures—the Sanhedrin and then finally Herod Antipas and Pilate. There is a reason he was crucified as "King of the Jews" and not merely "Anointed One of God." He was seen as a political threat, even if he was a nonviolent messianic figure, unlike various Zealots.

At the beginning of this chapter we considered in some detail Jesus' relationship with his cousin John the Baptizer, and we noted as many differences as similarities between the two. Jesus was not as much like an Old Testament prophetic figure as John. He performed miracles and proclaimed good news and violated purity laws in order to reach the least, the last, and the lost, even banqueting with the bad. Even John had doubts about Jesus and did not know what to make of some of his behavior. Jesus chose to reveal his identity in his own way and on his own schedule. Why then did Jesus dodge certain kinds of acclamations of himself, silence others, and insist on calling himself the Son of Man, over and over again? In our final chapter in this volume we will address this question.

NOTES

1. John Updike, "The Gospel According to Saint Matthew" in *Incarnation: Contemporary Writers on the New Testament*, ed. Alfred Corn (New York: Viking, 1990), 8-9.

2. An exception might be the Samaritans, who still exist in Nablus, but there would be debate as to whether they should be called Jews or not.

3. Corban is an offering to God in fulfillment of a vow.

4. The Mishnah is the first recording of the oral law of the Jewish people, as championed by the Pharisees. It was written around A.D. 200 and is considered the first work of Rabbinic Judaism. This quotation is taken from Sanhedrin 11.3.

5. Julius Wellhausen, *The Pharisees and the Sadducees: An Examination of Internal Jewish History*, trans. Mark E. Biddle (Macon, Ga.: Mercer University Press, 2001), 45.

6. For a full discussion of Jesus' views of money see Ben Witherington III, *Jesus and Money* (Grand Rapids: Baker Books, 2010).

7. These offered praise and thanksgiving to God.

CHAPTER FOUR

ENTITLED TO A NAME— SON OF ?

Jesus was the man who fits no one formula, no single name.

—*Eduard Schweizer*

Name-calling these days is seen as inappropriate conduct. In antiquity, however, name-calling was precisely how a person figured out who they really were, because identity was shaped and determined by what the group said about you. Jesus experienced both negative and positive name-calling throughout his ministry, but when he finally cleared his throat and called himself names, he preferred the title of Son of Man. As we shall see in this chapter, he tended to deflect or replace names when others, even demons, called him by titles he did not prefer. In this chapter, as a window on Jesus' self-understanding and how those who related to him viewed him as well, we are going to review some of the names Jesus was called and then how he referred to himself.

JESUS AS SON OF MARY

Whereas today we may well be proud to be called a son of our mother (though I can't recall anyone ever addressing me as "son of Joyce"), in an ancient patriarchal culture this was widely perceived as an insult. Even well after the death of a father, a son would still be called by his father's name, for instance Simon bar-Jonah (Simon son of Jonah). This makes what we find in Mark 6 and the parallels in Matthew and Luke all the more striking.

Jesus is in his hometown, and his hometown folks feel resentment at something or some of the things Jesus says in his inaugural synagogue address there. Mark 6:3 reflects various attempts to take Jesus down a peg or two, as the assumption seems to be that Jesus, with his "wisdom," has gotten too big for his britches, so to speak. First, it is said that Jesus is a *tekton*, which means an artisan—someone who works with stone or wood. The translation "carpenter" is probably too specific for our ears. Then it is asked if this isn't "the son of Mary?" Now this question is surely pejorative (even more pejorative than calling someone a "Mama's boy" today) in light of the last portion of verse 3: "And they took offense at him." Indeed, it could be as strongly pejorative as calling someone today an S.O.B. But by calling Jesus the son of his mother, it may suggest that they think they know Jesus has dubious origins, immoral origins, and doesn't deserve to be called son of Joseph. Even if Joseph was long dead (and it seems likely he was indeed deceased at this point or he would be mentioned), the tradition was still to call a man by his father's name. They do not do this in this story. It is worth noting that Jesus does not call himself "son of Mary," and in the two stories in John where he could have done this (John 2 at Cana and John 19 at the cross), he actually calls his mother "woman" rather than mother, which should be compared with Mark 3:21, 31-35 where Jesus says whoever does the will of God is his mother. In short, "son of Mary" is an example of naming Jesus in a way that is pejorative, a way that Jesus does not name himself, and this is telling when it comes to Jesus' self-understanding. He will readily call himself the Son of Man (son of humanity) but not Son of Mary.

JESUS AS SON OF DAVID

We are all familiar with the genealogy in Matthew 1, which has as part of its purpose to show that Jesus comes from the royal line of David. He is "son of David" in that sense. What is odd about the genealogy from a modern point of view is that it is Joseph's genealogy, not Mary's, and of course, Jesus was not literally "son of Joseph" as the Gospels freely admit. What one needs to know in addition is that in early Judaism, when a man adopted someone as his son and legitimate heir, he was legally entitled to his adoptive father's genealogy, hence there is no sleight of hand in giving Jesus Joseph's genealogy in Matthew 1. But a more interesting question is, What did Jesus think about the whole Jewish tradition of the Messiah (Christ) needing to be a descendent of David?

One of Jesus' most interesting teaching moments is found in Mark 12:35-37 and the parallels in Matthew and Luke. Jesus is teaching in the Temple precincts during the last week of his life, and he asks the question, "Why do the teachers of the law say that the Messiah is the son of David?". This presupposes, of course, that the crowd listening to Jesus knows that this is a dominant interpretation by teachers, particularly in Judaea. This line of interpretation is entirely understandable in light of 2 Samuel 7 and the promise made to David, and the revision of that tradition in 1 Chronicles 17:11-14 where the collective reference to "your offspring" becomes a specific reference to "one who shall be from among your sons." It is interesting, however, that the first clear reference to the phrase "son of David" only comes in the warrior Messiah passage in Psalms of Solomon 17:23.

Jesus seems to question this whole line of thinking by citing the Psalms, particularly Psalm 110:1. For Jesus' question to be a pointed one, one has to accept that David himself is speaking as the author of Psalm 110. There then appears to be a discrepancy between what these Jewish teachers are saying about the Messiah and what David himself suggested about the Messiah in Psalm 110, particularly at its beginning. It is worth noting that we have found no evidence of general speculation about the Messiah in early Judaism based on Psalm 110:1. This idea seems to come from Jesus, and we find that sort of discussion furthered in early Christian documents such as Acts and some of the Epistles.

Notice that Jesus does not directly refer Psalm 110:1 to himself, though this seems to be implicit. Jesus is not being coy but rather allowing the audience to draw their own conclusions after careful reflection on the matter. The point seems to be to show the inadequacy, not the inaccuracy, of the tradition that the Messiah would be the son of David. The point is to make clear that the Messiah is much more than just a descendent of King David. He is, in fact, David's Lord and is called Lord in the psalm (presupposing a messianic interpretation of this psalm).[1]

In sum, Jesus is challenging the adequacy of simply viewing the Messiah as a descendant of David, though not denying that tradition itself. Jesus is suggesting that the Messiah might be a much more exalted figure—in some sense the Lord of David himself, suggesting his supernatural origin and dignity. It is interesting that in Mark 14:62 Jesus will use the same text again to talk about his return from heaven as the Son of Man who will come to judge the earth in the future. This short passage then tells us a lot about what Jesus thought about the character of the Messiah without coming out and directly identifying who this Messiah is, though it would appear much is implied.

There are a variety of "son of David" texts in the Gospels that require a different sort of interpretation than we might expect. Obviously, in David's own time, *the* son of David turned out to be none other than Solomon. There appears to have been a son-of-David tradition in Jesus' own day that used the phrase to refer to a figure that seemed like Solomon in some important way. For instance, in Matthew 12:22-23, we hear about Jesus healing a demon-possessed man, which healing raised the question could Jesus be the son of David? Why this question? Because it was widely believed in Jesus' day that part of the wisdom Solomon obtained in his own day was the wisdom of cures, including the wisdom for performing exorcisms using the title son of David.

This helps explain why a blind man sitting on the side of the road might call out to Jesus as son of David—that is, as a latter-day Solomon figure—for healing (see Mark 10:46-52). What is especially interesting about this whole tradition is that in the Old Testament there are no stories about the healing of a blind person. We hear a promise in Isaiah 61 that someday it will happen when the Messiah comes, but we have no narratives about it happening prior to the coming of Jesus. In both Matthew 12:22-23 and in Mark 10:46-52, the story is about a blind person (even though the Matthean story is also about a demon-possessed person). Consequently, Jesus is seen to have the wisdom for cures of even things that the Old Testament never records cures for, hence the title son of David. But again, Jesus himself makes nothing of this title directly. He does not apply this to himself directly. He does, however, repeatedly call himself something else: Son of Man

JESUS AS SON OF MAN

In the rest of this chapter we must take time to discuss what Jesus could have meant by calling himself "Son of Man," a very odd phrase on any showing. In the Greek, the phrase is literally "*the* (not *a*) son of humanity" rather than simply the Greek word for a male. By the Middle Ages the phrase was taken to simply indicate that Jesus was truly human as well as truly divine; but in fact, it is doubtful this is the meaning of the phrase in its original Jewish context.

If there is one thing on which almost all New Testament scholars agree (which, in itself, is remarkable since there is little unanimity among biblical scholars on anything), it is that Jesus called himself "the Son of Man." And he did so repeatedly in all sorts of contexts and settings. But what does this seemingly innocuous phrase mean? Was Jesus just affirming he was a human being, something that would have seemed obvious to everyone? If so, why is this Jesus' repeated self-designation of choice?

One of the reasons scholars are confident that this phrase tells us a good deal about how Jesus viewed himself is that later Christian tradition made little or nothing of the phrase! Search as you may the rest of the New Testament outside the Gospels, or early Christian literature in general, and you will almost never hear Jesus being called "Son of Man." There is one reference to Jesus as "Son of Man" in Acts 7 on the lips of Stephen in a highly Jewish context, and then nothing for the rest of the big book of Acts. There are no references to Jesus as "Son of Man" anywhere in the letters of Paul—nowhere! And Jesus is called Christ or Lord hundreds of times in Paul's letters and elsewhere in the New Testament. What all of this evidence convinces scholars of is that there was no propensity of later Christians to slap the Son-of-Man tag on Jesus as a way of explaining his identity. No, Jesus apparently is the one person who insisted on calling himself this. Here we are at the very epicenter of how Jesus viewed himself during his ministry. Although he does not deny he is God's Son or the Savior or the Messiah, what he prefers to call himself in season and out is "Son of Man."

In order to understand this, we must start with some background, namely Daniel 7:13-14, which is not in Hebrew but in Aramaic. There we hear about one like a "human being." And yet this mysterious figure is also unlike any normal son of humanity in various ways. Let us begin with the observation that Daniel 7 needs to be seen in the context of the visions of the previous chapter in Daniel. There are four beastly empires and rulers referred to, followed by Daniel 7, which refers to a humane empire with a ruler who appears like a human being. In a general sense, the author is suggesting that the final human and humane empire and emperor will supplant and be a big improvement on the previous beastly and evil empires and rulers, but there is much more.

In antiquity, a king was seen as the head of the kingdom, the representative of his people, and God's agent to his people, and so an intermediary in both directions. What is being promised in Daniel 7:13-14 is that God's people, through their representative, will finally overcome all their oppressors and will rule as God intended. There was in fact a long development of this whole Daniel 7 tradition before Jesus came along, as can be seen in 1 Enoch. Jesus is interpreting himself and his ministry in light of a long messianic and end-time tradition about the final ruler of God's people, the final ruler on earth.

Daniel 7:14 seems clearly enough to be a royal investiture scene. The Son of Man is presented before God, known as the Ancient of Days, and extraordinarily he is given an eternal kingdom, one that will last forever, and he is even worshiped in this scene! What sort of person could rule forever in an earthly kingdom and rightly deserve worship? This is especially a pressing question for the strongly monotheistic Jewish context in which such a vision is related. Who could this Son of Man be? It is instructive to contrast this tradition with what we find in 2 Samuel 7 where David is promised a whole line of royal descendants. Here there is reference not to one mortal ruler after another, with son replacing father again and again, but rather a final everlasting ruler. It becomes clear the closer one examines Daniel 7:13-14 that this "Son of Man" figure is both human and yet more than human. He is no mere mortal, for he rules forever and is worthy of worship, without any objections from the Ancient of Days, and on top of all this, he will judge the earth, something that elsewhere in the Old Testament is a task reserved for Yahweh himself.

I would suggest that these very rich and complex verses in Daniel 7:13-14 provide us with the proper background for understanding Jesus' self-consciousness and self-expression. He saw himself as human and also as more than human. He was not just another in the line of David, to be replaced at some point by a further person in the line of David. Jesus had no heirs, and more to the point, he expected no successors![2] Armed with this knowledge, let us turn to key sayings of Jesus, with one more preliminary reminder: Jesus called himself *the* Son of Man, not merely *a* son of man. The definite article that occurs over and over again is significant. It means "I am the aforementioned (in Daniel 7) Son of Man." Jesus interprets himself, and encourages others to interpret him and his ministry, in light of the Danielic vision.

Let us start with Matthew 8:20 and Luke 9:58. This proverbial saying is of course familiar, "foxes have holes, and birds of the air have nests, but the Son of Man has nowhere to lay his head." This is obviously a saying from during the period of Jesus' itinerant ministry, and it suggests not merely that he doesn't have a permanent home of his own anymore, though that was true, but also there is an edge to this saying that suggests he was a controversial figure not welcome in many quarters, and apparently not welcome for long anywhere—even in his home town. The saying suggests Jesus had already experienced some rejection, but rejection by whom? Here it is important to remember that Jesus had once called Herod Antipas, the ruler of Galilee, "that fox" (Luke 13:32). Could Jesus be deliberately contrasting himself with Herod, who had built two royal cities (Tiberius and Sepphoris) for himself, not to mention his palace in Jerusalem? It is possible.

Luke 9:44b is our next text of interest, which tells us that the Son of Man will be manhandled, handed over (by someone) into other human hands. As we will see shortly, this warning of imminent danger and arrest finds fuller expression when Jesus begins to make some predictions about his coming demise. For now we should remember that at various points Jesus warned his audience that he was the man born to die.

One of the most famous Son of Man sayings is Mark 10:45: "the Son of Man did not come to be served, but to serve, and to give himself as a ransom for the many." This saying, which combines ideas of Isaiah 52–53 and Daniel 7:13-14, is important for a host of reasons. First, it may well explain to us Jesus' reticence to call himself anything other than "Son of Man." Jesus came as God's servant, and as such he called himself by humble and self-effacing terminology. He did not come like a king to be served but rather to serve. Indeed, he came to give up his life for others. The term *ransom* suggests that those for whom he died were in some kind of serious captivity or bondage. They were slaves to someone or something and needed rescuing. Second, this giving of self was substitutionary—the one dies in the place of the many, thereby ransoming them. Third, the term *many* does not describe God's intent to only save the elect. The contrast here is not between *many* and *all* but between the one who dies for sins and everyone else who does not—the many. Ironically, Jesus is the one person for whom Jesus did not need to die. He was not a sinner, though he was tempted like us in all respects as the author of Hebrews tells us.

A further crucial Son-of-Man saying is found in Mark 14:62. The context is crucial here. Jesus is appearing before the Sanhedrin, and the high priest has brought the proceedings to a climax, asking Jesus, "Are you the Messiah, the son of the Blessed One?" Jesus replies in the affirmative but immediately changes the terminology saying "And you will see the Son of Man sitting at the right hand of God and coming on the clouds." It is this last saying that is the straw that breaks the camel's back, and it calls forth the cry of blasphemy and the high priest's tearing of his robe as a symbol that blasphemy has been spoken. Jesus is claiming to be that future coming Son of Man, and even worse, he is claiming he is the human and divine figure mentioned in Daniel 7 who will one day come on the clouds of heaven to earth to judge the earth, including those who seem to be judging Jesus at that very moment. This of course is a bridge too far for these authorities and leads to Jesus being handed over to Pilate.

What we have seen thus far is that Jesus early, middle, and late in his ministry called himself the Son of Man in various important settings and in various theologically loaded ways. But this chapter would not be complete if we didn't examine perhaps the most crucial of the Son-of-Man sayings delivered at Caesarea Philippi to the disciples when they were outside the Holy Land itself! For this we turn to Mark 8:27-33 and the parallels in Matthew and Luke. Here again context is crucial. Caesarea Philippi was north and just beyond the borders of Galilee, in Herod Philip's territory. Indeed it had become his capital city. It was an odd city for a Jew to choose as a capital, as it had been a Greco-Roman city called Banias or Panias, named after the Greek god Pan originally. But Philip had renamed it after himself and after his sponsor Caesar, hence Caesarea Philippi. Naming and names were always important in that world, and Jesus chooses this locale to reveal his name and mission.

There is more background needed to understand the full force of Mark 8:27-33. First, there were cult statues of various pagan gods at the heart of this city, which Herod, though partially Jewish (and partially Edomite), had left standing in their shrines. But more recently an imperial cult temple dedicated to Augustus had been built on this same site. Here many gods and saviors were honored and worshiped in the true pagan tradition. It was in this pagan setting that Jesus asked (and answered) the question about his identity. Second, in Mark's presentation of the Gospel, there have been no Passion predictions up to this point in the narrative—nothing about the Son of Man having to die. It cannot be an accident that once the who question is partially answered by Peter at Caesarea Philippi, it is then and then only that Jesus says that the Son of Man must suffer many things and be killed, and on the third day rise. In fact, once the who question is answered, four Passion predictions follow, climaxing with the saying we have already considered in Mark 10:45. One cannot understand why Jesus had to die, Mark is suggesting, until one first knows exactly who Jesus is. Last, these shrines, including the one to Augustus, stand right next to a cave called the cave of Pan, but also there was a tradition that one of the tributaries of the river Styx, the river into the underworld, could be found there. That is to say, the cave of Pan was seen as one of the gates of Hades. This becomes crucial in the Matthean version of this story at Matthew 16:13-23.

The story begins simply enough with Jesus asking, "Who do people say that I am?" The disciples respond that some think Jesus is one of the prophets, perhaps an end-time Elijah figure, or even perhaps John the Baptizer come back from the dead. But then Jesus points his finger at his disciples, having heard the opinions of the crowds, and asks, "But who do *you* say that I am?" Jesus is not asking this because he is having some sort of identity crisis. This is the way people in ancient collectivistic cultures talked about themselves—indirectly. They asked others who they were. Notice that Jesus speaks of himself in the third person, calling himself "the Son of Man."

Peter clears his throat and says, "You are the Messiah, the Son of the living God." Now it is clear that Jesus affirms this assertion, but we notice once more how quickly Jesus turns the terms of discussion to the Son of Man. In the Matthean telling of the story, Jesus blesses Peter for what he says, gives him the nickname "Rock/Rocky," and tells him that the keys to the Kingdom will be given to him and that the gates of Hades (perhaps Jesus even pointed to the cave at this point) would not prevail against his community. Jesus is talking about his community never dying out and Peter playing a crucial role in the inaugurating of that community. But then the story takes an unexpected and dramatic turn—for the worse in some respects.

Jesus then tells his disciples, once the *who* question has been answered, that the Son of Man must indeed suffer many things, be killed, and on the third day be vindicated by God, rising from the dead. Peter is horrified by this pronouncement. In his mind an executed Messiah was a contradiction in terms (notice Jesus doesn't mention crucifixion here, the specific form of punishment he would endure). So Peter rebukes Jesus for this dark saying, but Jesus returns the favor calling his Rock "Satan," saying, "Get behind me, Satan." Peter may understand something about the identity of Jesus, but he does not yet understand the mission— that Jesus is the man born to die. And it is at this juncture that the first half of the Synoptic story comes to a dramatic conclusion with the disciples both informed and confused, both knowing Jesus is a Messiah figure but having not figured out his mission and final destiny. In our next study in this series, we must look at the events that led up to the dramatic last week of Jesus' life, and then the last week of Jesus' life where all manner of things happen, and the story has a surprise ending in several parts.

IN SUM

We have examined more facets of the life of Jesus, specifically his Galilean ministry, and some of his self-presentation. One of

the common reactions to studying Jesus and his life in this fashion is that it is noticed how very Jewish Jesus was and how very
different he is from most of us who live in the twenty-first century. In actuality, we would find the world of Jesus just as odd and
different as Jesus seems in his original context. In that world, they
did things differently. The past, as one person once said, is like a
foreign country. But if we want to really understand Jesus himself,
and not just the Jesus we have created in our pious imaginations,
we must come to grips with the strangeness and differences we
find in the Gospels.

The implications of this study for our faith are varied, and they
are important. The first thing to say is that a responsible historical approach to the data in the Gospels presents us with a Jesus
who viewed and presented himself as both human and yet more
than merely mortal—as the Son of Man foretold in Daniel 7.
There is no escaping the fact that Jesus viewed himself as more
than just another prophet, even a prophet like John; more than
just another healer, even a healer like Elijah; more than just a
sage or wise man like Solomon; more than just the messianic figure du jour. Jesus expected no successors or peers and saw himself
as distinct, unique, in various ways.

The second thing to say is that whereas the Jesus of history and
the Christ of faith are indeed one and the same person, and there
is continuity between the one and the other, the Jesus of the
ministry is not yet the risen Lord, has not yet atoned for the sins
of the world. In other words, we must take seriously that Jesus has
a story, including a history and a career, and the story in the
Gospel has a sequel as well, as a text like Philippians 2:5-11
makes clear. The Jewish Jesus of history becomes more than just
a messianic figure; he assumes the role of risen Lord over the
church and the world. The point I am making is that Jesus
assumes different roles at different points in the trajectory of his
preexistence, his life, and his existence in heaven (and returning
to earth thereafter). He has not yet come to judge the world, but
he will one day. He has already died on the cross for our sins.
There is a before and after to Jesus' story, his life, his titles, and
this makes perfectly clear that history matters when we evaluate

Jesus. He is not merely the plastic Jesus on the dashboard of our lives, a sort of Gnostic figure who was never fully or truly human. He is also more than the one to whom we pray and in whom we trust. While Jesus is more than the historical Jesus revealed in the Gospels, he is not less than that figure, and that figure is the person in whom we place our full faith. But there is another reason to know Jesus as well as we can. He taught us to be like him, to take up our cross and follow him.

In this study we examined at some length the Sermon on the Mount, of which the basic premise is: "This is how I behave (says Jesus), and so should you." It is a call to Christlikeness to be peacemakers not warmongers, to be meek not weak, to hunger and thirst for righteousness like zealous Jesus, to be poor in spirit without being mean-spirited, and so on. The Sermon on the Mount is not a utopian ethic, it is a reminder that we become what we admire, that we emulate whom we follow, and that God gives what he commands, by his grace and in his good time. The Sermon on the Mount reminds us that both our thoughts and our deeds, both our attitudes and our actions, matter in life, for we are like cities set on hills, and people are watching to see what sort of light comes forth from us.

It is inescapable that Jesus was a controversial figure. He had many controversies with his fellow pious Jews—Pharisees, Sadducees, Zealots, and others. He was in various ways a revolutionary without being a violent Zealot. He was always in trouble or stirring up trouble—what church would hire him today as their minister? Jesus was hardly innocuous or the "gentle Jesus meek and mild" of some hymns. The reason we may think him innocuous or harmless is because we have been infected with a slight case of Jesus that is preventing us from getting the real thing. Jesus will challenge all our categories, our well-worn assumptions, about our life, our politics, our religion, our whole worldview. If the least, the last, and the lost are on the way to becoming the foremost, the first, and the found, then the kingdom of God works very differently than the beastly kingdoms of this world.

We finished this study with a close reading of the story of Jesus and the disciples at a pagan city called Caesarea Philippi. In some ways it is much like the pluralistic, multireligious world in which we live. And yet it is precisely in such a pagan place—a place where gods, humans, and lords are honored and worshiped—where Jesus chooses to reveal both his identity and his destiny, both his majesty and his humility, both his humanness and his more than humanness, both his death and his resurrection. At Caesarea Philippi there was a preview of coming attractions that even the most perceptive of disciples could hardly comprehend or grasp. The danger for disciples ancient and modern of Jesus is not that they believe too much about him and in him, but they believe too little, and trust him too little as well. Jesus insists he is the fixed point around which the whole world turns, he is the change agent who takes us from the promise of salvation to its reality, and he is the one servant who died as a ransom for all of us. Jesus himself presents us with a scandal of particularity that we cannot get around.

It is not our job to whittle off the hard edges of the story of Jesus to make him more acceptable to one and all. If the world of humankind is to do an about-face as it speeds headlong toward oblivion, it needs a Jesus that gets in its face and causes it to face both who we are as fallen human beings and who he is as the unique Son of Man. It is, in the end, our job to see him more clearly, love him more dearly, and follow him more nearly, day by day, as the old *Godspell* song says. We don't need to know everything about Jesus, either the historical Jesus or the Christ of faith, to follow him. We need to know only enough to begin the journey and trust where Jesus leads us. In our next study, we will take the next step in the journey with Jesus, but already at Caesarea Philippi, we can hear the old gospel tune's strains—"on a hill far away, stood an old rugged cross, the emblem of suff'ring and shame."

NOTES

1. In its original setting, the psalm may well have meant the following: "The LORD" (that is, God) said to "my lord" (that is, David). The speaker in that case

would be the priest speaking about the King. Jesus, however, sees the speaker as David the king rather than as the priest. With David as the speaker, then both "the LORD" and "my lord" have to be someone other than David (that is, God and the Messiah, respectively).

2. For much more on all this see Ben Witherington III, *The Christology of Jesus* (Philadelphia: Augsburg Fortress, 1990), 238-62.